Distrust and Educational Change

PARENTS! 11, 12

Distrust and Educational Change

Overcoming Barriers to Just and Lasting Reform

Katherine Schultz

HARVARD EDUCATION PRESS
CAMBRIDGE, MASSACHUSETTS

Paperback ISBN 978-1-68253-297-3
Library Edition ISBN 978-1-68253-298-0

Library of Congress Cataloging-in-Publication Data

Names: Schultz, Katherine, author.
Title: Distrust and educational change : overcoming barriers to just and lasting reform / Katherine Schultz.
Description: Cambridge, Massachusetts : Harvard Education Press, [2019] | Includes bibliographical references and index.
Identifiers: LCCN 2018049658| ISBN 9781682532973 (pbk.) | ISBN 9781682532980 (library edition)
Subjects: LCSH: Educational change. | Organizational change. | Effective teaching. | Teacher-student relationships. | Community and school. | Trust. | Attitude (Psychology)
Classification: LCC LB2822.8 .S37 2019 | DDC 371.2/07--dc23
LC record available at https://lccn.loc.gov/2018049658

Published by Harvard Education Press,
an imprint of the Harvard Education Publishing Group

Harvard Education Press
8 Story Street
Cambridge, MA 02138

Cover Design: Ciano Design
Cover Image: "Reform in a climate of distrust" by Marianne Jansen Rollinson
The typefaces used in this book are Stone Sans and Minion Pro

To Nora, Danny, and Jenna,
who inspire me daily.
You are the future.

Contents

1

Defining and Identifying Distrust in Educational Settings

In the fall of 2015, a coalition of community activists initiated a thirty-four-day hunger strike to protest the closing of Walter H. Dyett High School in Chicago. This action shone a spotlight on the issue of school closures and their impact on local communities. The extreme response of calling for a hunger strike in response to a school closure illustrates the power and poignancy of unaddressed distrust in impeding educational change.

A HUNGER STRIKE AS A RESPONSE TO THE CLOSURE OF DYETT HIGH SCHOOL

Dyett High School is located in the Bronzeville community on Chicago's South Side, an area that has been the cultural hub for African Americans since their arrival as a part of the Great Migration from the South nearly a century ago. Dyett was the last open-enrollment neighborhood school in an area that has seen rapid demographic shifts due to new housing policies and a dramatic decrease in school-age youth.[1] Sometimes called comprehensive schools, open-enrollment schools admit all students in a neighborhood, rather than selecting students according to certain criteria. After a four-year phaseout that diminished its resources, prevented new students from enrolling, and led teachers to leave, Dyett High School had closed its doors the prveious spring with a graduating class of just thirteen students. Some students who had attended Dyett left for other schools, often traveling miles to reach them. To fulfill the requirements needed for graduation, the remaining students were required to take online courses—including an online gym course—to supplement the few courses still offered. Teachers departed in the middle of the year, afraid that they would not find a job if they stayed any longer.

Parents and community members protested that without this open-enrollment school in their community, there would be few options for their children; the nearby schools included a selective high school, a contract school run by a private operator, and a school that was outside of the neighborhood attendance zone. To attract national attention and underscore their grievances against the district office, school board, and mayor, community activists called for a hunger strike. Twelve people refused to eat until their grievances were addressed; and the number of supporters went well beyond those individuals.

Chicago was no stranger to radical action in support of education. In the fall of 2012, an extended teacher strike had garnered unprecedented support by parents and community members. The following May, the district closed fifty schools—one of the largest number of school closings at a single time in the United States, affecting twelve thousand students—despite citywide protests and the occupation of buildings by parents. Some of the closed schools were replaced by charter schools, further fueling the anger and distrust of parents and activists who feared the loss of local control over their children's education. Adding to the outrage, the closed schools were disproportionally located in African American neighborhoods.[2] Although these events can be interpreted along multiple dimensions, I understand them as representative of the growing distrust between communities and district officials, two groups struggling to enact lasting educational change.

Although the distrust expressed by the community members toward the Chicago Public Schools (CPS) authorities was most visible, the mayor, the district's CEO, and the board in turn distrusted the vocal Chicago Teachers Union and the community activists. This reciprocal distrust should be understood in the context of a hierarchy and imbalance of power. The community was represented by several powerful grassroots organizations with a history of challenging the authority of the mayor and his school board. For instance, earlier that same summer, the Rainbow/PUSH Coalition, which was affiliated with the strike, challenged the district's proposals for closing schools and, in particular, their selection of which schools to close and which to expand. The Coalition's history of grassroots actions fed the reciprocal distrust in the debate over Dyett High School. The mayor and CEO wielded greater decision-making power and their solutions appeared to intentionally favor the participation of some members of the community over others. Naming the distrust on both sides—including the history, surrounding politics, local context, power dynamics, and interpersonal missteps that indicated a lack of respect for the dignity of individuals—might have made it possible to address the distrust through honest dialogue. Instead, there was an impasse that lasted for days.

DEFINING DISTRUST

Distrust is often defined as the absence of trust and is frequently equated with suspicion and doubt. In relation to education reform, it can be parsed in several different ways: as a disposition and characteristic of individuals; a set of behaviors or actions that promulgate negative reactions and feelings, including disconnection; or an attribute of particular contexts and institutional arrangements.[3] Typically, in conflict situations, parties distrust each other. The events that transpired in Chicago—which are emblematic of growing discord across the country in response to the privatization of schools and the rise of high-stakes testing as the primary form of student and teacher assessment—reflect the three types of distrust identified and elaborated on in this book: relational, structural, and contextual distrust.

Relational distrust is grounded in interpersonal relationships that are characterized by unpredictability and unreliability. It is the most frequently recognized form of distrust and often masks the other two forms of distrust: structural and contextual distrust. In other words, people often identify individuals and institutions as untrustworthy, when in fact, there are structural or contextual antecedents. The remedy for relational distrust in educational settings is often to simply replace the distrusted person or change the institution rather than to examine and address the political and historical causes of that distrust.

Structural distrust is connected to local politics and consequential decisions made by politicians and others in authority. Structural distrust is embedded in hierarchies and bureaucratic structures or policies and is characterized by an imbalance of power that undermines participation by local communities. This type of distrust often stems from top-down decisions.

Finally, *contextual distrust* arises from local interactions that have persisted over time, often between members of various ethnic and racial groups, and is also inflected by power. It is situated in the sociocultural, historical, and political contexts of schools and communities.

Although relational distrust often appears to be the most prevalent and the easiest to identify, the various forms of distrust are frequently interwoven. In fact, when relational distrust causes deep, enduring damage, it is almost always connected to one or both of the other forms of distrust. While simple relational distrust can sometimes be remediated by building trusting relationships, more enduring relational distrust demands that the political and historical roots of the distrust are addressed if there is to be lasting change. All of these dynamics were apparent in the conflict over Dyett High School.

RELATIONAL, STRUCTURAL, AND CONTEXUAL DISTRUST IN THE DYETT HIGH SCHOOL CONFLICT

The distrust that fueled the conflict over the future of Dyett High School had deep roots in local structures, conflicts, and relationships, and was influenced by larger social dynamics, including national reform movements. It thus could not be remediated simply by substituting trust for distrust; that is, by reaching out, building coalitions, or supporting collaborative actions, important as those acts can be. The hierarchical sources of distrust were rooted in the imbalance of power between the authorities who made decisions and the community members who had to live with them. Policy makers may have had more success in resolving the issues behind the strike and associated discontent by examining the history of distrust between the community members and the mayor that was based on conflicts over housing policies and other issues in this neighborhood. And beyond acknowledging distrust, those in power might have drawn on the knowledge and resources of the community itself to repair it. Lasting educational change only occurs when both parties grapple with the actions that engender distrust.

The Dyett strike was linked to past injustices experienced by Chicago's African American community and similar communities across the country whose schools have been consistently underfunded and neglected for decades. It was also connected to the vital importance of education in Bronzeville. As one of the leaders of the strike, Jitu Brown, explained, "Even when we were in slavery, black people fought for schools . . . Our ancestors evacuated the South to come here, to find a better life for their children . . . The institution that our ancestors fought for and won—we've got to reclaim it."[4] Such statements emphasized the the strikers' connections to larger social justice movements in which African Americans fought for control over their own schools, as well as other poverty-related issues such as adequate health care, jobs, and housing. In choosing to wage a hunger strike, protesters drew on practices African Americans have historically used to preserve their dignity while mobilizing in support of their deeply held beliefs.

Brown and his colleagues distrusted the CPS Board of Education's decision-making process, declaring that it was rigged against the community's interests. They sought to bring national attention to the decisions about their school as well as the plight of many schools that once served Chicago's African American and Latinx communities. The CEO and the board countered that the growing budget deficit, coupled with changing demographics, necessitated school closings. Both groups claimed that their solutions were in the children's best interests. Each group raised questions about the other side's ethics, values, and understanding of the situation.

The hunger strike ended after thirty-four days, with the strikers declaring victory in having drawn national and international attention to the inequities of an education system that neglected its working-class black and brown communities. Throughout the strike, the activists had repeatedly claimed that they did not trust the board members—who were not residents of their community and operated from a position of authority rather than local knowledge—to make decisions about their children.

The underlying distrust stemmed from the way that the board developed a compromise solution without the input of the hunger strikers, reflecting their allegiance to the mayor; the coalition supporting the strike claimed that the board's solution was put together too hastily and did not reflect the vision that the community had developed based on six years of deliberation. The community felt shut out of the decision-making process and silenced by it. Distrust was located in the structures that vested the power to make decisions in outsiders rather than in people with local knowledge.

Relational Distrust in the Closing of Dyett

Relational distrust is often personal and arises when an individual or group does not believe that the decisions or actions of other individuals and groups of people are based on a shared set of values or principles. Relational distrust was evident in nearly all of the interactions between administrators, teachers, parents, students, board members, and school district officials in relation to the closing of Dyett High School. The decision to initiate a hunger strike rather than to continue to engage in conversation illustrated the relational distrust the protesters felt toward the authorities and their decision-making processes. In trying to reach a compromise, the mayor, CEO, and selected board members attempted to address the distrust by claiming that their plan represented "the opportunity for a unique, world-class high school on the south side." The CEO of Chicago Public Schools, Forrest Claypool, explained, "Working with community partners, we arrived at a solution that meets multiple needs: creating an open-enrollment neighborhood high school, producing an enrollment stream that can weather population changes, filling the critical demand for an arts high school on the south side and working with education leaders to create a technology hub."[5] This compromise, however, was initially not acceptable to the activists. Importantly, it did not name and address the district's distrust of the community groups. In addition, it did not take into account the depth of that distrust and its structural and contextual roots, including the race and class positions of the protestors. Rather than explicitly naming the source of the discord, the district leaders proposed a solution that silenced the group that had brought the problem to the fore. While the compromise may have addressed some of the community's surface concerns, it intentionally excluded the protestors from contributing to the solution and did not recognize the dignity the hunger strikers sought to assert in their decision to embark on a hunger strike.

Dyett's closing affected many individuals, while also reflecting a larger social pattern of school closures. Community activists across the country have claimed that school closures and charter school expansions disproportionally affect African American and Latinx students. When a school closes, a set of community relationships is lost and community members's lives are significantly affected. Schools contain histories of individuals and families, orienting people to their geographic locale in deeply personal ways and serving as an anchor for the community. The relational distrust that stemmed from the closure of Dyett High School came from both a decision-making process that ignored this history, including the individuals who lost their school.

Structural Distrust in the Closing of Dyett

The relational distrust among the stakeholders involved in the set of decisions concerning Dyett High School was tightly connected to both structural and contextual distrust. The decision-making powers and processes of the mayor-appointed school board were a critical component of the structural distrust. The board members and school district officials responsible for this school closing—along with a large number of closings in 2013—made the decisions *for* rather than *with* the community. Structural distrust reflects hierarchical decision-making in which those in power make decisions for those in less powerful positions, often ignoring their dreams or demands. If authorities, such as the school board, simply address the relational distrust without articulating the structural causes, distrust will persist. In Chicago, the hunger strikers' demands went beyond a distrust of the relationships between the community and the authorities and the anger over Dyett's closure; they were also connected to a fight for local control of the school board. When the strike ended, the organizers turned their attention to this new battleground.

Unlike 98 percent of the school districts in the United States and all the other districts in Illinois, Chicago has never had an elected school board; its members have been appointed by a variety of methods since 1872 and, since 1995, solely by the mayor, after the state legislature gave the mayor full authority over the Chicago Public Schools. Among several important findings in their examination of the history and record of the Chicago Board of

Education, Pauline Lipman and her colleagues concluded that "[m]ayoral control and Board structures and processes limit public input and democratic accountability. The Board has been markedly unresponsive to outpourings of public opposition to its policies and essentially indifferent to advice and proposals of parents, teachers, and others with expert knowledge and who have a primary stake in students' education."[6]

Mayoral control of school boards is often associated with top-down decisions and heightened one-way accountability measures, such as the use of test scores to evaluate teachers, school closures in response to low student test scores, and the application of business models to education. In the United States, participatory democracy is thought to be a hallmark of local governments and institutions.[7] Thus, in contrast to appointed boards, elected school boards are associated with greater democracy and the public role in the governance of public schools. When public institutions limit local participation or govern without seeking input from local stakeholders, there is often distrust in the decision-making processes and in the people who make the decisions.

Appointed school boards, first introduced in the 1980s and 1990s, are generally imposed on struggling districts by governors as a solution to persistent poor financial management or concerns about academic achievement, generally measured by scores on tests given by the state. Several other reform measures that have been developed at the federal, state, and local levels seek to achieve the same goals. As I discuss in chapter 3, these reform measures are often undercut by the distrust that they engender. For instance, the reforms that are typically supported by appointed boards and designed to promote school change often create distrust among teachers, parents, and community members who are unhappy with decisions made by people who are considered outsiders and unaware of the needs of the children and youth served by the schools.

Contextual Distrust in the Closing of Dyett

In addition to the structural distrust that shaped the interactions between the community and the board, the history and politics of the district were integral to the contextual distrust experienced by the community activists. The hunger strike arose from distrust tied to the local context of Chicago

Public Schools and specifically to neighborhood surrounding Dyett High School. A report prepared by Public Agenda in 2012 identified a legacy of distrust as the first of five tensions that characterize the response to reform by the Chicago community of parents, teachers, and educators: "Although CPS has recently taken steps to incorporate community concerns and improve communication, many parents, teachers and community leaders bring a long history of skepticism and distrust to the table. They wonder whether recent attempts to reach out are genuine and whether the District has any long-term commitment to them."[8]

Adding to their distrust of the board, the community felt a strong desire for a high school in their neighborhood that reflected their own historical legacy of artists and activists. In the 1920s, Bronzeville was well known because of its many prominent African American artists, entertainers, and activists, including dancer Katherine Dunham, journalist and social activist Ida B. Wells, musician Louis Armstrong, author Richard Wright, and poet Gwendolyn Brooks.[9] The high school itself was named after Walter H. Dyett, a music teacher and violinist in the Chicago Public Schools, who taught such well-known musicians as Nat King Cole and Dinah Washington. The community did not feel that the compromise proposed by the board took account of this history and legacy.

The board's decision to close Dyett because of the area's changing demographics increased the distrust of the community, who felt that their neighborhoods had been consistently undermined for years. They also felt disenfranchised from the political process that failed to rebuild affordable housing, as promised, leading to the closure of their high school. Their distrust in the political process was tied to a history of political exclusion in several arenas, a diminishing of public services, and the quality of their lives.

The responses to the Chicago school closings might have led to a more enduring solution valued by all constituents, if the contextual distrust was clearly articulated by both the strikers and the school authorities, if the dignity of each group was recognized, and if the response was more explicitly tied to local and historical contexts. The coalition that supported the strike included community organizations such as Kenwood Oakland Community Organization (KOCO) and the Journey for Justice Alliance (J4J), two groups with long histories of activism in Chicago. Both groups have historically positioned themselves against Chicago's recent mayors, including Mayor Rahm Emanuel and his administration, which may have led the mayor and board to construct a solution that did not include them in the compromise. Naming and acknowledging the distrust as an issue and exploring the local contours of the distrust, including its historical and political antecedents, would have made an amicable and lasting resolution to the perceived educational injustice more likely.

In selecting their form of protest, the hunger strikers looked to history. Hunger strikes have long been used by African Americans and other disenfranchised groups to call attention to injustices in the United States and around the world. Africans starved themselves during the Middle Passage to America to protest their enslavement. Imprisoned Freedom Riders staged hunger strikes to protest their wrongful imprisonment. In Chicago, on Mother's Day in 2001, fourteen mothers and grandmothers in Little Village, a Latinx section of Chicago, staged a hunger strike that led to the opening of a new social justice–focused high school in their Mexican community, Little Village Lawndale High School. The strikers demanded that the district fulfill its promise to build a new high school to serve their growing neighborhood, whose only high school was overcrowded and crossed two gang territories. This action was launched for similar reasons to the Dyett hunger strike: in response to a situation where families felt betrayed by the CPS officials. The distrust expressed by the strikers was not simply anger at the mayor and other officials, it reflected a history of disappointment and harm by authorities.

* * *

To create positive and lasting change grounded in trusting relationships, one strategy for those in charge is to uncover, acknowledge, honestly name, and directly address the genesis and sources of the distrust. If this is not done, the solutions will be fleeting, because the persistence of distrust can impede positive change and reform. The Chicago school board had a plan to address its fiscal difficulties by closing schools that they identified as underenrolled and underperforming. The Bronzeville community, for social and historical reasons, wanted to hold on to a neighborhood school. They felt that it was the last vestige of connection to and identity with their once-flourishing section of Chicago. They valued an open-enrollment school that allowed all youth in the neighborhood to have access to education.

Each side distrusted the other's motives and actions for a variety of reasons. The board tried to indicate their own trustworthiness by suggesting a compromise: a school with a slightly different focus. The community, represented by the hunger strikers, read the offer as a dismissal of their demands and their stated interests. An analysis of the distrust of the hunger strikers would have encompassed an examination of the local history and context and also the national debate about school closings and privatization that grounded this conversation, a recognition of the structural distrust of an appointed board whose interests extended beyond the community, and an observation of the political, historical, and social contexts of the protest. Instead, there was a failed attempt to build relational trust with the hunger strikers.

DISTRUST, TRUST, AND EDUCATIONAL CHANGE

The three kinds of distrust I elaborate in this book, which are reflected in the narrative of the fight for Dyett High School, are prevalent in schools and across education systems in the United States. They are key to understanding why educational reform is so difficult. Teachers were once almost universally trusted by their students' parents. Today, all too often, teachers feel distrusted by both parents and administrators. They are often worried that they will be negatively judged and evaluated by their students' test scores, rather than trusted to teach children using their own experience and assessments. Likewise, principals are often concerned that their schools will be judged negatively by falling test scores—to the extent that several have cheated by changing students' test answers in attempts to hold onto school funding.[10] These actions undermine the perceived value of teachers as professionals and principals as instructional leaders who observe, guide, and provide opportunities for teachers to continuously learn and grow to improve teaching and learning. An atmosphere of distrust makes this kind of learning nearly impossible.

Students and parents, as illustrated in the Dyett example, frequently feel unheard, their perspectives unsolicited or devalued in the race to privatize schools, balance budgets, and standardize teaching, curriculum, and assessment. The push to reform educational systems has ignored the ways these "reforms" create disequilibrium for the stakeholders who are necessary to enact the change, which in turn leads to distrust and prevents the change necessary for educational institutions that serve all students well.

Trust is an essential component in every teaching and learning interaction. Learning—on the part of students, teachers, and administrators—takes place only in an atmosphere of trust. Although trust is often linked to the smooth functioning of schools and classrooms, the role and prevalence of distrust in larger educational settings is rarely examined.[11] If trust is necessary for people to learn and change, the presence of distrust, or actions that lead to greater distrust, prevents change.

Trust can be understood as the glue in human relationships. To learn and to change, and to enact the reforms that are necessary to improve educational opportunities for students, it is essential to risk not knowing and make oneself vulnerable in order to truly learn as an individual, an institution, or a system. At the same time that learning something new is always built on what a person or institution already knows, it also always involves holding knowledge loosely and being open to the transformation of familiar ideas or the absorption of new ones; the process of opening oneself up to change requires a measure of trust. When teachers, students, and schools are tightly monitored—in other words, distrusted—it is impossible to imagine a successful process of change and the likely result is that the educational reform will fail.

Given the essential importance of trust in nearly all aspects of teaching and learning, the ubiquitous presence of relational, structural, and contextual distrust in educational institutions and among administrators, teachers, students, and parents is alarming. A climate of distrust makes change difficult, if not impossible, and works against the publicly stated desire for school reform and change. There is a fundamental tension between the trust required for teachers, principals, or other educators to experiment with new ideas and the current policies and practices, which engender distrust.

THE PLAN OF THE BOOK

There is a general consensus that current US education reforms are failing. There is little evidence that educational opportunities for *all* students are getting better; many would say they are getting worse, especially for youth in the highest-poverty urban and rural areas. In this book, I describe the ways that many current education reforms engender distrust and how all too often reforms fail because unaddressed distrust prevents their successful implementation. I propose that the strategies we as a country have chosen to enact change undermine precisely those characteristics that would enable successful reform. While much has been written about trust, little has been written about distrust in educational contexts.[12] To explore how distrust is both created by and is an obstacle to reform, this book is organized around three detailed narratives, illustrating relational, contextual, and structural forms of distrust. Each of these narratives is based on detailed field notes I collected while working in each context. In addition, I relied on field notes collected by graduate students working with me in two of the contexts (Chester and Lebanon), interviews with a wide range of participants, and published documents from a wide range of sources.

I bring to this book my understanding as a teacher, scholar, and activist committed to providing opportunities for all children and youth to learn in contexts and through interactions that recognize their human dignity, as well as the historical injustices that have shaped educational opportunities in the past. I have worked for almost forty years as a classroom teacher, professor, researcher, and dean in P–12 and university settings. During the time that I taught and worked in leadership positions in these varied settings, I always worked to improve educational opportunities for all children and youth.

In the next three chapters, I explore the relationship between one particular form of distrust and educational change. In each narrative, I played various roles as both observer and participant. The stories include distrust of me as an outside researcher and of the institutions I represent, including their historical and political relationship in the community. In each of these contexts, I also experienced moments of trust and possibility.

Relational distrust is foundational to all forms of distrust. In chapter 2, I illustrate how relational distrust works at the district level through an historical account of the churn of superintendents in Oakland, California, over the past eighteen years. Despite the initial trust accorded to superintendents who came from Oakland and those who were outsiders, I describe how, in each case, the local community came to distrust them. The public's distrust was directed toward the superintendents as individuals in the form of relational distrust; the analysis of the political, racial, and historical roots of the distrust was missing from the dialogue. In other words, in each case, structural and contextual distrust that lay underneath the relational distrust of an individual were ignored, and the superintendents were blamed for the failure of the reforms. Because the superintendents unsuccessfully addressed the structural and contextual components of the community's distrust when they entered their positions, they were unable to enact the lasting change they desired.

The narrative of chapter 3 is located in Chester, Pennsylvania, and illustrates structural distrust. Chester is home to one of the poorest and lowest-performing districts in the state. It has repeatedly drawn the attention of the national media for its inability to pay its teachers and the teachers' decision to work without compensation. In each instance, at the last minute, the local court has ordered the state to give the district money to prevent this from happening. The financial distress and academic decline of the Chester Upland School District led to a state takeover in 1994. I was a member of an Education Empowerment Board or school board, appointed by the governor, which oversaw the district between 2007 and 2010. Despite our efforts to build trust with individual community members, we discovered that the distrust in the district was structural, located in the existence of an oversight board that did not trust the community to run its schools. Our efforts as an appointed board to enact lasting change ultimately failed, in part because we focused primarily on building trust rather than directly addressing the distrust embedded in the structural and political nature of our appointment.

In chapter 4, drawing on professional development work I conducted in Lebanon with Palestinian principals, I explore the historical and contextual nature of distrust. Palestinians live in Lebanon in a climate of insecurity and distrust, and the principals' distrust came from the particular local, historical, economic, and political contexts of living and working within the refugee camps of Lebanon. They brought their political and factionalized relationships to the workshops and were unable to break out of the patterns of deep distrust to engage in the collective problem-solving processes that we introduced. In addition to building trust, it became clear that we needed to directly acknowledge the contextual distrust that shaped their actions. Professional development is a key lever to educational change. All too often, professional development is conceptualized as a one-time training session that does not take into account the local context and the complexity of enacting new ideas. This chapter explores these ideas in a particular context in Lebanon, drawing parallels to the United States.

In chapter 5, I use the lens of distrust developed in the initial chapters to critically examine how distrust has shaped several key educational policies, as well as their fates. In this chapter, I briefly review the recent history of educational reform in the United States to explore the consequences of the three types of distrust for efforts to shift educational practice. Through an analysis of key moments of educational reform over the past few decades, I argue that the failure of each reform movement to address structural inequalities is connected to its basis in blame and a deficit perspective that ultimately lead to distrust. I begin by describing two sets of reforms: policies that focus on the achievement of equal opportunity and access to schooling for all students and strategies that emphasize global competitiveness through greater accountability and curricular reform. I argue that the failure of these reforms led to a third set of policies: the current market-based reforms. As in the other chapters, I argue that the inattention to the role of distrust in educational change has contributed to cycles of failure that are evident in the history of educational reform.

In chapter 6, I describe approaches to education change that have addressed distrust. Here, I argue for education reformers to resist quick fixes and pay attention to the elements of time and collaboration in the reform process. In addition, I discuss how essential it is to recognize the dignity of children, teachers, and communities in order to address distrust. Through contrasting stories of reform in New Jersey—in Union City and Newark—I examine what happens when distrust is addressed through slow, thoughtful work with local teachers and in classrooms as occurred in Union City, as compared with Newark's approach of bringing in outside consultants and attempting to make changes quickly without community input. In addition, I provide examples that illustrate several ways to address distrust including: honoring the knowledge teachers bring to teaching and policy making; building on children's capacity for learning; creating solutions with the community defined broadly rather than imposing solutions from the outside; and creating educational spaces that honor people's dignity.

* * *

Across the United States and throughout much of the world, there is a general feeling of dissatisfaction with the educational opportunities available to children and youth, particularly those living in high-poverty urban and rural areas. The public often casts the blame for the failure of P–12 schools on teachers, families, public schools themselves, and, most recently, schools of education. Social scientists widen the list of causes of the failing educational system to include poverty and social inequality. Responding to the belief that schools are not serving all children well, policy makers have offered numerous strategies or educational reforms, which the general public often views with great skepticism. These strategies come from policy makers who may or may not have expertise or experience in schools and, increasingly, come from wealthy foundations and individuals. Beneath the discussion of possible solutions lies persistent and somewhat intractable feelings of distrust. The distrust is directed at various people and institutions and expressed in the blame voters ascribe to US public schools for failing to provide a high-quality education for all children and youth, particularly those living in high-poverty communities. Education policies are often based on blame and distrust and, in turn, all too frequently perpetuate more distrust.

Social science surveys in the United States have documented a steady decline of trust in the past several decades. Recent polls show that the

United States is becoming a less trusting society, with youth more distrustful of government, educational institutions, and religious institutions today than in our recent past.[13] This is hardly surprising, as there has been much written and discussed about the pervasive distrust in the United States and around the world, especially of politicians and governmental leaders. In the United States, people have ascribed Donald Trump's successful bid for the White House to his ability to connect to the public's distrust of government and public institutions. Positioning himself as an outsider, he captured this sentiment and translated it into several of his proposed policies, including building a wall between the United States and Mexico to keep out immigrants, as well as his assertion of the unreliability of many public institutions, including the media and the justice system. At the same time, during the campaign, the media regularly reported that both Hillary Clinton and Donald Trump were among the most distrusted political candidates to run for president of the United States.

Whether the prevailing distrust has arisen from the economic crisis of 2008 or other factors, there is little doubt that it is a destabilizing force that extends to schools and educational contexts. And while distrust is a much-discussed issue in political circles at this moment in the United States, it is a product of decades of decisions and relationships between those with political power and those without resources in this country. Likewise, the various instances of distrust in education are more visible today, yet they have deep historical roots that require sustained and collective work. This book posits that the desire to quickly build trust through activities or a focus on relationships is simply not enough. It is strategies that foster human dignity, while acknowledging and working toward reparation of each of the three types of distrust, that can help school leaders, parents, policy makers, and students to reenvision a path forward for educational change.

2

Relational Distrust and the Barriers to Change

In 2017, Oakland, California, school superintendent Antwan Wilson announced his departure after just two and a half years in the position. It was the latest departure in a rocky history of outsider superintendents. Wilson's abrupt resignation led many local residents and organizations to demand that the school board appoint an Oakland native as his successor. Several community leaders asserted that the experience of growing up in Oakland and understanding its community was more important than any other standard qualifications the next superintendent might possess. Many vocal community members strongly advocated for a local superintendent, signaling the paramount importance of trust in this decision. It was important that the next superintendent would remain in the position for more than a few years. To do so, many people felt, the superintendent would have to know the city, including its racial politics and history of activism.[1]

During the previous eighteen years (2000–2017), there had been ten OUSD superintendents (including interims), only three of them (including one interim) local.[2] The most recent, Wilson, had come from Denver; and many people, including teachers, parents, and school administrators, felt that he had attempted to impose ideas from another city onto Oakland, without considering the differences between them. He had brought a team of administrators from Denver to implement his new policies, replacing people with a history in and deep connections to the community, while significantly enlarging and restructuring the district office. Wilson entered a district that had long been struggling with financial distress, with an equally long history of distrust among key stakeholders. Many of the people I interviewed in Oakland—including past and current board members as well as key staff who left the district before the end of his term—pointed to Wilson's disinclination to appreciate its unique historical circumstances, his impatience to enact change without consulting the community, and his exacerbation of fiscal problems by increasing the number of high-salaried senior administrators as factors that contributed in signficant ways to an accelerating spiral of distrust.[3]

The churn of superintendents has become a common phenomenon in urban districts across the United States, and a deterrent to sustained progress for many of them. The Oakland community's demand for a local superintendent reflected a central theme that had animated the district for many years: a persistent fear that outsiders sought to take advantage of and control the direction of the district and its struggle to improve educational quality and equity. The story of how the district and its community reached this focus on hiring an insider is a story of relational distrust: the distrust of outsiders and the (perhaps blind) trust in insiders.

Many conversations about distrust begin with relational distrust, which is embedded in our everyday lives and interactions, and is an increasingly central component of public discourse across the world. We frequently hear about politicians who are distrusted by their constituents and the public at large, as well as institutions that are not trustworthy. Notably, relational distrust has recently been growing in the United States. A 2014 Gallup poll reported that only 32 percent of Americans had confidence in what Gallup has pinpointed as the fourteen key institutions, such as churches, Congress, the military, newspapers, the Supreme Court, and public schools. To zoom in on one relevant specific: in 1975, 65 percent of the surveyed population had a "great deal" or "quite a lot" of confidence in public schools; in 2017, only 36 percent shared such confidence.[4] In 2017, the Pew Research Center found that public trust in the government was lower than it had been since 1958, while the General Social Survey (GSS) reported that the fewest number of Americans agree with the statement "most people can be trusted" than any time in the last forty years.[5]

However, if we closely examine what people say when they talk about relational distrust, particularly with regard to educational change, its genesis nearly always lies in the larger historical or political context. For instance, one of the most controversial decisions that superintendents make, especially in recent times, is school closures, as illustrated by the opening story of Dyett High School. Usually the individual superintendent is blamed for the decision, when it is often the consequence of longer-term decisions (e.g., financial mismanagement over decades), past political choices (such as the simultaneous development of charter schools and small autonomous schools), and myriad other factors. In other words, though people may blame the failure of a certain educational policy on the individual implementing the change, the genesis of their distrust of that individual often has its roots in historical precedents and politics and is located in particular cultural contexts.

As I detail in this chapter, Oakland residents have tended to blame individual superintendents for the failure of specific policies, when in fact, underneath the veneer of relational distrust focused on individuals, it is a story of structural distrust, deeply bound up with the fierce racial politics of the district, and of contextual distrust grounded in historic events specific to the city that shaped current actions and memories, including a persistent and reccurring fiscal crisis.

Oakland was not always a struggling school district filled with distrust, though the last fifty years may make it appear that way. Its first school opened in the 1850s. In 1909, a Chamber of Commerce guide to the city boasted, "Oakland's chief pride is its public school system and the fact that her schools rank among the highest in the United States. No more modern school buildings can be found in any city in the United States than in Oakland."[6]

Despite its positive beginnings, both insiders and outsiders have recognized for many years that the Oakland Unified School District has been in a state of distress since the turbulent 1970s. Some point to the 1973 assassination of Marcus Foster, the first African American superintendent in Oakland and a champion of community participation in the schools, as one of the turning points. Foster was highly regarded by many Oakland residents, teachers, and administrators, and his needless death caused many people to lose faith in the prospect of turning around the schools. Furthermore, during the 1960s and early '70s, Oakland experienced increasing rates of gang violence and a growing prevalence of drug use. As in most other urban centers, a sharp rise in poverty had a significant impact on all aspects of education in Oakland. In 2000, a report from the Pacific Research Institute noted: "With dismal achievement scores, classroom horror stories, administrative chaos, and the Ebonics controversy, the Oakland Unified School District (OUSD) has become the poster child for the failings of public education in California and across the nation."[7] In February of 2000, *Education Week* reported, "Long regarded as one of the state's most troubled districts, Oakland struggles with a huge population of poor students, abysmal test scores, fiscal mismanagement, lamentable school maintenance, and transient leadership."[8]

By 2017, despite several attempts at reform and numerous innovative and experimental programs, both insiders and outsiders described Oakland as a district that was resistant to change and improvement. The wide range of residents whom I interviewed described the district as characterized by distrust at multiple levels: between teachers and school leaders, as well as between local communities and the district office, with a particular focus on distrust of the superintendents charged with addressing the challenges.

Since 2000, in response to persistent poor school conditions, district office insiders, local political leaders, and outside foundations have brought nearly every popular educational reform to Oakland. Initiatives, reorganizations, and support efforts have included: small schools; state takeover; appointment of superintendents with management training from the Broad Superintendents Academy; reconstitution of school faculty and staff; high school redesign; scripted curricula; various forms of privatization, including charter schools; new avenues for recruiting teachers, such as Teach for America; full-service community schools; and more. In most cases, senior administrators introduced the reforms, generally without meaningful engagement with the community in either their design or implementation. As with most districts, there have been and continue to be several exemplary schools with extraordinary teachers and students, and many moments of celebration and success. But these bright spots are too often overshadowed by a pattern of persistent distress. Although a multitude of reasons have been broached for the district's challenges, as well as many proposed solutions, a majority of the schools—especially three of the comprehensive high schools located in the highest-poverty areas of Oakland—have not made sustained, significant progress for many years.

One of these schools, Fremont High School, is located in a high-poverty area of Oakland known for a history of gang activity. It stands three short blocks from International Boulevard, where there is a visible presence of teenage sex trade workers, a thriving drug market, and a growing homeless population. When Fremont opened in 1904 with 130 students as Union High School Number 4, it was considered a college preparatory high school with a strong academic program. At that time, its population was predominantly white and working class. In the late 1960s and early '70s, Fremont experienced the same kind of unrest that coursed through many urban high schools. Its location in Oakland meant that it was also a site for student organizing by members of the Black Panther Party.

During these years, however, it remained a desirable school for residents of its surrounding community.[9] But beginning in the 1970s, the school was confronted with the increasing poverty of its neighborhood, the racial tensions of the rapidly changing student body, and the impact of a struggling district that has continually faced fiscal crises. Those challenges persist. In recent years, the combination of extreme poverty, shifting racial dynamics, and fiscal challenges at the district level have left the school without adequate resources, creating a climate for distrust that pervades the district as a whole.

In this chapter, I review the educational policies of OUSD superintendents from 2000 to 2017 to illustrate the role of relational distrust in the failure of educational reform or change. I use the case of Fremont High School to exemplify how distrust played out in a specific context. I provide this account largely from an outsider perspective, augmented by the insider perspective I gained in my role from 2010 to 2014 when, as dean of the School of Education at Mills College, I co-led the Oakland Education Cabinet (OEC) with Superintendent Tony Smith and Mayor Jean Quan. The

OEC, whose meetings I chaired, comprised district and community leaders invested in the success and future of the Oakland educational system. As well as providing a close-up view of one period of Oakland's ongoing struggle to fix its schools, this role gave me access to school district officials, school board members, community members, teachers, and administrators during that time period and beyond.

DENNIS CHACONAS (2000–2003): FROM OPTIMISM AND REFORMS TO FISCAL CRISIS

Many people trace the current crisis of the Oakland Unified School District, and of schools such as Fremont, to the administration of Dennis Chaconas and the subsequent takeover of the district by the state in 2003. Chaconas, an Oakland native, was appointed by the school board in 2000, which believed that he could implement change that would turn the district around. Chaconas had been a teacher and principal in Oakland, and a superintendent of Alameda, a smaller neighboring district. His appointment was made over the objections of recently elected mayor Jerry Brown, who saw education reform as a cornerstone of his vision for the revitalization of Oakland, and powerful state senator Don Peralta.

Chaconas's story was a quintessential Oakland success story. He went to Oakland schools, including Fremont High School, and was able to attend college because two of his high school teachers paid his first semester of tuition. His parents had also attended Oakland schools, though both dropped out before they completed elementary school. The knowledge that he was from the community prompted many people to be optimistic about his understanding of the district and his ability to turn it around.

Like many of his predecessors and the superintendents who followed him, Chaconas was immediately confronted by significant fiscal troubles. Although he was an Oakland insider in many respects, especially because of his educational history, he was considered an outsider by the local politicians because he was not chosen by them and did not display political saavy. He focused his attention on students and teachers rather than the larger financial picture of the district, which was plagued by dropping enrollment numbers tied to a significant decrease in state funding. A history of patronage added to the fiscal troubles; Chaconas discovered that many people on the payroll did not even work in the district. As superintendent, Chaconas replaced or transferred about two-thirds of the principals and gave teachers a 24 percent pay raise, which people assumed would slow the high teacher turnover rate. (Oakland salaries are still far below its neighboring districts.) While these changes were embraced by many members of the school community, engendering good will and a modicum of trust, they also led to a huge deficit and ultimately to bankruptcy, prompting an abrupt state takeover of the district. Oakland was one of six districts taken over by the state in 2003 for financial reasons.

The Small Schools Experiment and Fleeting Trust

At the time Chaconas was appointed as superintendent, various groups had introduced parallel reforms in Oakland to address stark inequities across the district, while giving principals more autonomy. These included a nascent movement to create small public schools and a growing interest in bringing charter schools to the district. Each of these reforms was reflective of national trends in K–12 education at that time. Local community organizing groups promoted them, with the support of Mayor Jerry Brown.

The small schools movement began as a response to the significant disparities between the largely successful white middle-class schools in the Oakland hills and the struggling schools located in Oakland's flatlands, which were populated by mostly Latinx and African American poor and working-class children. Partnering with the Oakland Communities Organization (OCO), a grassroots organization of community and religious leaders, Latinx mothers organized to develop a proposal for change.[10] Organizers from OCO created a map that vividly illustrated the disparities: not only was there a gap in the student achievement data, but there was a notable disparity in the size of the elementary schools. All of the schools in the hills were small, with much larger and underresourced schools in the flatlands. No new schools had been built in thirty years in the district, and overcrowded schools were commonplace, especially in the flatlands. Although their initial strategy was to start new small charter schools, OCO quickly realized that a more sustainable and larger-scale solution would be to work with the district to break down the larger schools in the flatlands into smaller public schools.

The movement to create small schools started slowly and then quickly increased its scope with support from the district, including an oversight district office, a local school reform organization, and external funding. The initiative was approved by the school board in 2000, the same year that Chaconas became superintendent. To insure the success of this community-initiated reform, OCO held sixty action meetings across Oakland, with thousands of parents attending.

The small schools movement also shifted the ways that the district involved parents in school governance. At the instigation of the OCO, the district included parents on the school design teams and placed a parent liaison in each school, thus both supporting parents and involving them in school governance. Organizers and educational activists hoped to use this reform to leverage large-scale change in the district from the ground up. In a yearlong planning process, a local education reform group, BayCES, applied for and received a $15.7 million grant from the Gates Foundation to build a small schools "incubator" to coach the design teams, which were composed of principals, teachers, and parents. National attention turned to Oakland.[11]

However, as often happens in high-poverty school districts, rather than focusing on a single reform, administrators moved forward with several different—and ultimately competing—reforms at the same time. The unanticipated growth of charter schools and the introduction of open enrollment in the district jeopardized the initial success of the small school movement. Each of these reforms drew students away from the district-run schools in the flatlands and had a significant impact on the viability of the small schools, which were strategically located in this higher-poverty area as a way to improve the existing public schools.

Several charter schools opened in areas adjacent to the new small elementary and high schools, and thus drew from their student populations. As a result of school funding formulas and the fact that charter schools draw their students unevenly from traditional public schools (e.g., they may attract third-graders from five different schools, leading to small classes in each school, but too many students in a single school to justify its closure), the increase of charter schools in Oakland, like much of the country, led to severe consequences for the district budget. In addition, the open enrollment plan allowed students to select any school within the district and, as a result, many high school students who had access to transportation transferred to the better-resourced and higher-prestige schools in the hills.

The move to create autonomous schools, which encompassed the development of both small public schools and charter schools, embodied the central elements of contextual and structural distrust in Oakland at the time: race and money. Race plays a role in nearly all politics and political decisions in Oakland. Most of the newly created small schools were located in the growing Latinx neighborhoods, which meant that the African American community was largely excluded from this reform. As a result, while the white, Asian, and Latinx communities generally embraced the small school movement, much of the African American community initially rejected it because it did not affect—or help—their schools. The charter school movement reflected similar racial dynamics and fiscal consequences. From the beginning, the support for charter schools in Oakland varied along racial lines, depending on the geographic location and residential neighborhoods where the schools were located, as well as the local politics of school closings connected to the opening of new charter schools, often leading to structural distrust. Many of the newly created charters schools started in predominantly African American neighborhoods, initially garnering more support from that community. In the end, both fiscal realities and racial dynamics, along with enduring issues of distrust, contributed to both the creation and eventual demise of the small schools.

THE STATE TAKEOVER PERIOD (2003–2008)

As the populations of particular schools and the district as a whole were shifting, relational distrust of Dennis Chaconas began to increase, due to the district's growing debt and questions about human resources issues.[12] In 2003, without advance notice, State Superintendent of Public Instruction Jack O'Connell fired Chaconas, appointed Randall Ward as the new superintendent, gave the district a $100 million emergency loan, and, overnight, turned the elected school board into an unpaid advisory board. After the fact, Chaconas acknowledged that he had focused too much on academics rather than paying attention to the financial condition of the district. It is likely that he also did not pay enough attention to state-level politics. He explained that he spent too much of his tenure as superintendent keeping city and state elected officials and their various requests at bay: "I ran the school system for the kids and not for the adults. There are people who had an ax to grind and they saw this as an opportunity to take over."[13]

State takeovers often stir community anger at the notion of governance by distant and uninformed political appointees. Oakland was no exception. The African American community was particularly unhappy about the elimination of local control. But the state, which was viewed as the ultimate outsider to the district, was only one element of the new outside control of the district. Ward, who was not an Oakland resident, was selected in part because he was a graduate of the Broad Urban Superintendents Academy, an organization created by educational philanthropist Eli Broad, who had funded Jack O'Connell's recent campaign. Over the years, Broad's mission has been to reform urban school systems, with a goal of training at least one-third of US urban superintendents. The academy teaches prospective superintendents a specific set of management strategies that were counter to many of Chaconas's practices, such as an emphasis on a top-down management style. One of Ward's first moves was to hire former colleagues from the Broad program—rather than from Oakland—to fill various positions in the district's central office. This move to fill district positions with outsiders is also typical of Broad superintendents.

The community initially greeted Ward with distrust because he was an outsider and because the state had appointed him unilaterally. However, at the beginning of his time in Oakland, Ward was surprisingly independent of the state power brokers. In his short time as superintendent of Oakland schools, he championed several community-initiated plans, including the continued growth of new small schools. Under his watch, for the first time in Oakland's history, the district raised large amounts of money from outside foundations such as Gates, Broad, and Dell, as well as Oakland-based foundations, including Clorox and the Kaiser Family Foundation. Although Ward officially resigned from his position in 2006, newspapers reported that he was fired because he did not follow the bidding of O'Connell and other politicians with regard to proposed real estate deals, such as selling school district properties to the city.[14]

O'Connell replaced Ward with another Broad Academy graduate, Kimberly Statham, who remained just a year. Statham was replaced with a third Broad graduate, Vincent Matthews, who served as superintendent until the state takeover ended in 2008.

Broad superintendents have a reputation for supporting privatization and "maximum disruption" as strategies to improve urban systems. There was speculation among many people in Oakland that the real intentions of the Broad superintendents were to use Oakland as a testing ground for their market-oriented ideas. There was little, if any, attempt to address the community's—and teachers'—deep distrust of the state's role in the district. Reflecting the mood of several members of the community, Sharon Higgins, a middle school parent coordinator and district employee wrote a letter charging that when the Broad superintendents came into power there was "a constant turnover of people, positions, and programs . . . with no end in sight." She claimed that the schools were "controlled by outsiders with no sincere allegiance to the well-being of our city" and that the state "has produced its very own Frankenstein monster." After this letter was published in the local paper, she was asked to resign.[15]

Ward's tenure as superintendent had both short- and long-term fiscal consequences. He made several visible decisions that enraged members of the community, such as closing low-performing schools and supporting their replacement by charter schools. As Ward explained, "We set up a free market."[16] California charter school laws, such as proposition 39 (also known as the "Smaller Classes, Safer Schools and Financial Accountability Act" and passed by voters in 2000), made it nearly impossible for districts to turn down charter schools. Twenty charter schools opened in Oakland between 2003 and 2009; the largest number opened during the state takeover period. Some were formed by coalitions of local residents who sought an alternative to the beleaguered public schools, others by charter management companies that ran chains of schools across the state and country. Given the precarious financial condition of the district, the charter schools had a fiscal advantage over the district-created small schools because of their ability to raise external funds from investors. As the small schools struggled to maintain enough variety in courses and sufficient staff, including counselors, students left them for charter schools with greater resources, as well as for district-run public schools in neighboring, wealthier districts. The drain of students added significantly to the district's budget shortfalls.

The final blow occurred in 2008, when the Gates Foundation declared that the small schools initiative was a failure in Oakland and across the country, shifted its attention from small schools to high school reform, and withdrew its financial support. Without the additional foundation money, the district struggled to maintain such a large number of small schools, each with its own administrative structure. Gates's withdrawal of support increased community distrust of money and control from outside foundations, as well as concerns for the welfare of the small schools. Many people continue to claim that the sudden withdrawal of Gates funding led to the demise of the small school movement in Oakland.[17] The status of the Gates Foundation as an institution with no vested interest in Oakland led to a generalized distrust of outside foundations as agents of reform.

The community's embrace of Dennis Chaconas as a local superintendent stands in clear contrast to the rejection and distrust of the three superintendents who served during the state takeover. Despite Randall Ward's initial success, members of the community largely dismissed all three superintendents because they were outsiders appointed by the state rather than chosen by a democratically elected school board. Their connections to the Broad Foundation and their decision to bring in people and ideas from Broad conflicted the local community's desire to manage their own schools. In other words, while community members directed their anger at Ward and his successors, their frustration—manifested as relational distrust of individuals—was in fact grounded in a structural and political distrust of the state's interference in local schools, of foundations that did not necessarily have Oakland's best interests in mind, and of outsiders, for a host of historical reasons.

Looking back on the period of the state takeover, former OUSD superintendent Robert Blackburn, who was severely wounded when Marcus Foster was assassinated, reflected that the state had treated Oakland "like an absentee landlord with slum properties," adding that the state takeover "was ill-advised and badly executed . . . As an educator, I'm embarrassed and ashamed, and as a parent and citizen, I'm outraged."[18] The district emerged from receivership $89 million in debt, with a $40 million structural deficit.

TONY SMITH (2009–2013): A RETURN TO LOCAL CONTROL

In 2009, when the state returned OUSD to local control, the district's debt had grown, due in part to the dramatic decline in enrollment from 50,000 to 38,000 students, which meant that it received less money from the state. In particular, the enrollment of the large comprehensive high schools had dropped precipitously. To further exacerbate the situation, as a result of the small schools initiative, despite the decrease in enrollment, the school district had opened more schools than they had closed during the period of state control, and Oakland now had 101 traditional district schools, and thus a ratio of students to schools that was far higher than neighboring districts. In addition, during the state receivership, the number of charter schools had more than doubled from 15 to 33. Ward closed 14 traditional public schools during his three years as superintendent and opened 13 charter schools. By 2009, Oakland had the highest percentage of students enrolled in charter schools in the state.

Tony Smith, the first permanent, locally appointed superintendent after state takeover ended, was selected by the newly elected school board. As a graduate of UC Berkeley rather than the Broad Academy, with several years of experience in the Bay Area, he was warmly welcomed by many members of community, in part because of his ability as a white superintendent to talk honestly and passionately about race and inequality and his commitment to putting resources into addressing economic and racial disparities.

Smith's lasting contribution as superintendent was to launch a full-service community schools initiative that many people considered to be one of most ambitious initiatives in the country. Smith planned to transform the district office and every aspect of school operations through a holistic frame of community schools focused on the whole child. According to this plan, everyone, from school nutritionists to reading specialists, would work to address the educational, social, and emotional needs of all children, while community-school liaisons created services that extended beyond the school day, such as school-based health and counseling clinics.

Twenty-seven schools were identified as full-service community schools within the first few years of the initiative that began in 2010. Smith worked closely with community and political leaders such as Jerry Brown, now governor of California, to develop and implement the community schools plan, bringing community members together to develop an ambitious five-year strategic plan with the community schools initiative at its center.

The community schools initiative was based in part on the fact that, as Smith explained at the time, an African American child born in West Oakland, in the flatlands and just two miles away from the predominantly white Oakland hills was "1.5 times more likely to be born premature, seven times more likely to be born into poverty, two and a half times more likely to not be vaccinated when they enter kindergarten, four times less likely to read at grade level by grade four, and six times more likely to be pushed out or to drop out of school before they graduate . . . That basically ends up with African Americans born in West Oakland having 15 years less life expectancy than white kids two miles away."[19] During Smith's first year as superintendent, sixteen students in the district were murdered. The community schools initiative was meant to address this set of dire conditions by coordinating social services within the schools.

Soon after Smith announced this ambitious vision and began implementation plans, he was confronted by the funding crisis and, in particular, repayment of the $100 million loan made at the beginning of the takeover. To address this debt, in 2011, Smith announced plans to close several under-enrolled schools and to merge the small high schools, reversing the reform that had broken up the large comprehensive high schools. While enrollment had begun to stabilize, the number of students in the district was 30 percent less than it had been in 2000, due to the growth of charter schools and other demographic shifts, as described above. Smith's logic was that by decreasing the administrative costs of small schools, the district could spend more money on its youth. One board member observed that Smith was also partly motivated to dismantle the small schools and recombine the high schools because the small schools reform was perceived to benefit mainly the Asian and Latinx communities, leaving out the African American communities.

Predictably, the 2011 proposal to close schools was met by outrage from several community factions. Many months of loud protests—at school board meetings, in front of the schools slated for closure, and throughout the city—ensued. The protests coincided with the growing momentum of the Occupy movement in Oakland, and a group mainly composed of white anarchist activists who used Occupy tactics to make their point brought their protests to Smith's home and confronted him at his children's soccer games. Parents living in neighborhoods with shuttered schools worried about which schools their children would attend. At the time, district officials admitted that as many as 20 percent of students might leave the district due to the closures.[20] While Smith's initial proposal was to close thirty schools over a few years, the district ended up closing just five elementary schools in 2012, all of them in the flatlands serving predominantly African American and Latinx communities. The small schools created by the division of the three large comprehensive high schools were also merged back together, and teachers in those schools were required to reapply for their positions as "teachers on special assignment" (TSAs).

Communities rarely embrace school closures, even when there seem to be few other alternatives to address a fiscal crisis. This time, community members aimed their anger at Superintendent Smith with little recognition of the political and historical context of the closures, including the financial situation that had created the problems. Before the vote on the school closings, the district had cut $150 million to try to balance its budget, but this was not enough to address the fiscal crisis. None of the factors in this crisis—the withdrawal of the Gates small schools money, the debt to the state, and decrease in state funding due to declining student populations—were directly Smith's fault; however, they did keep him from moving forward with his intended reforms, and when he left the district in 2013 because of family circumstances, after just four years (nonetheless, the longest tenure as superintendent since 1990), his plan to turn OUSD into a full-service community district had not yet materialized. Several schools had developed new and lasting connections to community services, and those innovations, such as school-based health clinics, have been sustained.

During his four years as superintendent, Smith's reputation eroded as faith in his leadership ebbed and distrust grew in the wake of the school closures and consolidation. His policy of requiring teachers in the three newly reconstituted high schools to reapply for their jobs as TSAs, added to the disapproval, especially from the teachers' union. Further, there were community members who distrusted his successful bids to obtain grants to support his ambitious agenda from both foundations and businesses. His support of several new charter schools added to the distrust and a perception that, like his Broad predecessors, he had moved the district toward a privatization agenda. While Smith had entered his position with trust from many sectors in the community, he left the district in a renewed atmosphere of relational distrust, directed at him personally, rather than located in the politics and history of the time period. His inability to garner community support for his various proposals meant that his vision for change essentially stalled when he left office.

ANTWAN WILSON (2013–2017): INCREASED DEBT AND GROWING DISTRUST

To address the crisis caused by the fact that there were too many schools for a declining student population, the board looked for a decisive leader with experience and success in school closures and turnarounds. Antwan Wilson, another graduate from the Broad Academy and a first-time superintendent, was eventually chosen for the position. While Tony Smith had stabilized the budget at the beginning of his tenure, he left the district on the brink of another fiscal crisis that the new superintendent would need to resolve.

Wilson came from Denver, where he had been a principal of a high-poverty school and an assistant superintendent charged with addressing the challenges of the eleven lowest performing schools in the city. He began his tenure in Oakland by bringing in a team from Denver, replacing several key staff and restructuring the central office, following the Broad model. (As one OUSD board member explained, reflecting community sentiment, Broad trains people not to trust anyone but their own people.) Wilson came to Oakland with seemingly little understanding of California laws and policies, including the budget limitations imposed by Proposition 13, or the history and politics of the Oakland community.[21] According to the board member, his motto was "You have to go fast in order to go fast."[22] People worried that he didn't have a well-thought-out strategy and initially moved too quickly.

Several board members characterized Wilson's approach as "command and control"; that is, he demanded order and allegiance. This style exacerbated relational distrust with board members, principals, community members, and teachers. Administrators and teachers feared retribution if they raised questions; several people pointed to examples of principals who were moved out of their positions because they either questioned the administration or did not clamp down on their teachers and demand order and compliance. While the distrust Wilson faced was certainly rooted in the community's historical distrust of outsiders, particularly those affiliated with external foundations such as Broad, people distrusted Wilson personally, a distrust exacerbated by his unwillingness to spend enough time understanding Oakland's complex political dynamics and history.

Wilson drove an ambitious agenda during his short time as superintendent, including an embrace of charter schools as district schools. As noted above, there has historically been tension in Oakland around charter schools, both because many Oakland residents do not perceive charter schools as public schools, and because charter schools drain resources from district-run public schools, contributing to the financial pressures experienced by districts. Yet at the same time, many parents, particularly from low-income African American and Latinx families, looked to charters as a safer, more orderly alternative to the district-run public schools.

Wilson proposed a multipronged approach for bringing charter schools onto the same playing field as the district-run public schools. Following the Denver model, he supported the idea of a single enrollment site where parents could view all schools—district-run and charter—on an equal basis. Supporters of this plan considered it more equitable, while detractors saw it as a way to give charter schools more visibility and traction in the district. For teachers with a long-term commitment to the district-run public schools, this move implied distrust of their work and contributions. The fact that the groups promoting the plan were funded by outside money, including wealthy philanthropists, only deepened the distrust. Wilson also embraced the portfolio approach to district schools, whose tenets are that the market will determine which schools—district-run or charter—will prevail.

One of Wilson's most ambitious initiatives, the Intensive Schools Support (ISS) program, was meant to identify schools that needed additional and targeted support to transform them into "quality schools."[23] The program was conceptualized by Gary Yee, the interim superintendent who preceded Wilson, and the board approved it at the same meeting in which they appointed him as the new superintendent. In the fall of 2013, Wilson and his team went to each of the five schools designated as low-performing to introduce the new ISS initiative. Following a process that district leaders had used in Denver, they invited applications or design proposals from charter schools and educators interested in starting a new school at any of the sites, as well as plans from the current school communities. It was notable to the community that Wilson embarked on this strategy of including charter schools as participants who could bid to redesign district-run schools before establishing knowledge, relationships, and trust in Oakland. Not surprisingly, these actions made it difficult for him to achieve his goals.

The ISS Process at Fremont High School: A Story of Escalating Distrust

The story of the ISS process at Fremont High School illustrates how relational distrust played out between the school staff and central administration. When I asked teachers and administrators to identify instances of distrust at the school, they often named individuals in the district office and the superintendent's top-down decisions. Although the unfolding of the ISS process at Fremont rapidly increased relational distrust, it was also intimately tied to structural and contextual distrust rooted in political and historical events that shaped the story of the school. As actual and perceived personal animosities in the relationship between the school and district went unaddressed, power dynamics inflected relationships and affected the contours of distrust over time. The history and interactional dynamics of Fremont High thus illustrate the interplay of relational and other forms of distrust.

In the fall of 2013, Antwan Wilson went to each of the five schools designated as low-performing schools to introduce the new ISS process. The three small schools on the Fremont campus had recently been recombined into a large comprehensive high school. Although the meetings at each of the other high schools were sparsely attended, with fewer than twenty-five people at each, and went relatively smoothly, there were over four hundred people at the Fremont meeting. This large turnout was prompted by growing fears of a takeover by outsiders, particularly charter schools.

Though the event began as an orderly meeting, it quickly devolved into a turbulent, emotion-laden event that went well into the night. One reason for the intensity of the response was that Fremont had relatively recently become a predominantly Latinx community, and the ISS reform was introduced by a new African American superintendent; thus the response was shaped in part by the legacy of tensions between these two groups at Fremont and in the wider Oakland community. In addition, unlike the two other schools, which had mostly new teachers, Fremont had a significant number of veteran teachers with a vested interest in the school remaining a district-run public school.

After the meeting, district officials, surprised at the size of the crowd, looked for an explanation and someone to blame for the disorder that ensued. They formally reprimanded the Latinx principal and community liaison, both of whom were from the neighborhood, charging that they did not have control of their community and had fomented disorder. The speeches by community members had made apparent their distrust of the central office and its policies. The district administration's distrust of the community was equally visible and strong, emanating from the superintendent and the officials from outside of Oakland who worked with him.

This meeting was one of many turning points for the school. The central message of the strong community presence was that the local families whose children remained in the school wanted—or more accurately, demanded—to be involved in the redesign process. They were opposed to the process being relegated to outsiders, underscoring their relational distrust of people who were not from their community. Most were adamant that they did not want a charter school to take over their school.

This new effort to transform the school through the ISS process should be placed in the context of the small schools movement in Oakland. It both mirrored and diverged from the small school design process. In each case, design teams for imagining—or reimagining—the school included administrators, teachers, students, parents, and community members. Importantly, however, the ISS design process was imposed by the district, whereas the small schools process was developed by and with the community. The ISS process assumed that principals, if not teachers, could be replaced; the small school movement was characterized by the creation and building (rather than rebuilding) of new schools. Finally, the small schools process was characterized by the hope for sustainable change initiated by community members; the ISS process was met with skepticism and distrust, in part because of the history of failure of reforms such as the small schools movement, as well as other top-down reforms. The school community saw the ISS initiative as one in a series of large promises with small returns, and many were extremely reluctant to venture down this path yet again.

Despite this initial distrust, a design team composed of teachers, student leaders, and a few community members was initiated in the winter of 2014. The district administration had given the design team a set of questions and tasks to address in order to initiate the transformation, and the team met regularly during the spring semester to respond to each of the detailed questions. It developed a comprehensive and complex design plan that was vetted by the students, teachers, and community members. However, the hopeful feelings generated by the design process faded as the plan, like many others, sat on a shelf.

Acknowledging distrust is different from assigning blame. A starting place for resolving these issues might have been to acknowledge that the relational distrust was reciprocal, rather than hoping it would dissipate with new leadership or new teachers. It is essential for all stakeholders to understand that trust can't simply be acquired through words, as one district official might have hoped when he asked teachers why they did not trust him. Building trust and addressing distrust depend on mutual actions and authentic opportunities for collaboration, not simply conversations and discussions. The process also depends on respect for teachers, community members, and students as people with relevant expertise. The distrust and disrespect experienced by the teachers and principals, as well as by the students, made it difficult for the school administrators or the district to enact the innovative change they sought. Any kind of lasting transformation depends on addressing and ultimately dispelling distrust, a process that cannot proceed quickly, and must address the historical relationships and political realities on which relational distrust is almost always grounded.

KYLA TRAMMEL-JOHNSON (2017): HIRING A LOCAL SUPERINTENDENT

In November 2016, Antwan Wilson announced his plans to leave Oakland for Washington, DC.[24] In the midst of another severe fiscal crisis—the district had a budget deficit of $30 million—he also informed the Oakland principals that their budgets were frozen. When Wilson left in 2017, auditors searched for causes of the crisis. They reported to the board that one cause was Wilson's decision to hire dozens of new administrators from outside of the district and pay them far more than their predecessors. In 2013, before Wilson became superintendent, only four Oakland administrators earned more than $200,000. Two years later, twenty-six administrators earned more than $200,000, and Wilson's total annual compensation package was more than $400,000, making him one of the highest-paid K–12 employees in the California public school system.[25]

Community trust of the district was at a low point. During meetings about the selection of Wilson's successor, community members demanded that the board hire a local superintendent. They rejected the initial slate of finalists because it included no candidates from Oakland. The locally elected board then put together a second slate of insider candidates. In the end, the board selected Kyla Trammel-Johnson, an Oakland native who had been a student, teacher, principal, and well-respected district leader in Oakland public schools. Community members largely received her favorably, despite the fact that she lacked experience as a superintendent and some of the skills required to run a large district, such as managing a large budget and negotiating with state politicians. As one community member put it, Oakland had no use for another Broad superintendent who saw their district as a stepping-stone to a more prestigious position.[26] The community's insistence on hiring a local superintendent underscores the relational distrust that had shaped the tenures of earlier superintendents; whether they succeed in this goal is still an open question.

CONCLUSION: ADDRESSING THE ROOTS OF DISTRUST

Superintendents are typically charged with bringing a vision and a plan to a district. Especially in urban districts in the United States, they are often confronted with large challenges frequently tied to insufficient resources, and recently, declining enrollment in district-run public schools. Too often, their vision revolves around the initiation of new programs rather than the continuation and elaboration of their predecessor's ideas, even when those ideas are promising. It seems nearly axiomatic that new superintendents want to start signature programs in their districts, rather than linking their work to the past practices.[27] This often results in disruption and discontinuities. If trust is associated with stability and predictability, this standard practice will lead to deepening distrust, especially when repeated—as it has been in Oakland—nearly every two years.

For education reform to take hold, it is critical to address the deeply rooted distrust that is so often present in school communities—whether superintendents are homegrown or come from the outside—even though this can be a slow and difficult endeavor. When new superintendents arrive in a district, they often—although certainly not always—initially attempt to build trust with the community and their staff. But the process of "building trust," which is often the language used in such efforts, often fails to begin with the recognition of distrust and of the historical patterns and relationships that have engendered it. Simply asserting the importance of building trust among constituents, like asserting the importance of stability and predictability rather than creating it, ignores the history of reform efforts, as well as the knowledge held by the community.

One of the lessons from the rapid turnover of superintendents in Oakland and the persistence of structural and contextual distrust, often disguised as relational distrust, is the importance of explicitly addressing distrust and, in the case of Oakland, to wrestle with the ways that it is embedded in fiscal issues and racial politics.

Following Dennis Chaconas's tenure as superintendent and the state takeover, every one of Oakland's superintendents attempted to address the the district's financial conditions. They each confronted a variety of roadblocks to lasting change. For instance, Tony Smith made significant efforts toward addressing the financial deficit he inherited. After unsuccessfully lobbying the state to forgive the payments on its $100 million loan and attempting several other measures to eliminate the debt, he turned to school closures as a cost-saving solution. School closures are nearly always controversial and protested by communities who fear that losing their school will lead to deterioration of their neighborhood and the loss of a community center. They rarely save a district money in the end. School closures also disproportionally affect poor African American and Latinx communities.[28]

Perhaps if Smith had focused on the distrust that accompanied his decision to close the schools, rather than emphasizing the facts (e.g., the poor fiscal conditions of the district and the declining enrollment) and found ways to speak to that distrust or, at a minimum, sought collaborative solutions that acknowledged the role of race and class in the calculus used to decide which schools were slated for closure, there may have been less public outrage. As it was, the angry reaction to the decision meant that it was difficult for Smith to enact his larger vision for the Oakland schools, including the creation of community schools. School board meetings became sites of conflict more often than of productive work.

In addition, Smith inherited a district with many young (mostly white) principals who had created or taken on leadership positions in the small schools. One staff member explained that they were each ambitious, looking out for themselves rather than invested in the district as a whole and for the long term.[29] As a result, the new leaders did not work together or trust one another. Smith needed to build buy-in to his solutions but instead, through his failure to understand or publicly articulate the depth of the distrust, moved forward with proposals that angered the community. In turn, they responded by distrusting him personally and making him the target of their rage.

It is instructive to wonder what might have happened if Smith had traced the historical roots of the financial crisis as well as the political decisions that went into the state's decision not to forgive the loan in his public conversations about school closings. What if he had used the distrust that had built up around the history of these actions as a way to bring people together to participate in finding solutions? Would it have made a difference to name the ways that distrust had built up over time, using that analysis to build collaboration?

Of course, one of the difficulties in that approach is that, in general, the public usually seeks simple solutions and people don't often listen long enough to complex ones. Smith was a gifted speaker, particularly when it came to identifying issues of race and inequity in Oakland. He deftly articulated the crisis in the education of African American boys in the district and harnessed support from the community and external foundations to address those issues through his African American Male Achievement project.[30] This engendered trust from the African American community.

But Smith did not bring that same force to the public discussions about the persistent debt in the district. He also did not clearly outline the costs to the poor African American and Latinx communities of the proposed school closures and consolidations. As a result of the unhappiness brought about by the decision to close schools and the growing climate of distrust, he had a difficult time moving forward with his vision.

Racial dynamics are often visible in interactions in Oakland. In several interviews, people emphasized that race is difficult to navigate in the district. As in many cities in the United States, the high level of poverty and lack of adequate resources mean that there are often public battles between various members of different racial groups for resources. A number of community members felt that, despite his position as the first African American superintendent in many years, Antwan Wilson did not take sufficient time to understand the particularities of the racial dynamics of Oakland. Not surprisingly, race plays out differently in Oakland than it did in Denver. Oakland has a reputation as an African American city, in part because of the prominence of the Black Panther Party headquartered there in the 1970s, highly publicized cases of police abuse against African Americans over the years, the 1990s Ebonics debate, among other significant events. Oakland also has a history of powerful African American leaders, continuing to today, even though the community has decreased in numbers and represents a smaller proportion of the population.

Many people see Wilson's central contribution to change or reform in Oakland as the promotion of the charter agenda through championing a common enrollment plan backed by a group called Educate78 and others.

Denver, where Wilson and many of his appointees had recently worked, had a common enrollment plan that listed district-run and charter schools on the same form that parents use to sign up for their children's schools. This idea divided the Oakland board and led to many contentious sessions. The focus of the discussion was often whether or not the plan would promote the growth of more charter schools. Led by the teachers' union, some of the constituents who insisted that the plan would do so, vehemently opposed it.

During Wilson's term, 25 percent of the students in Oakland attended charter schools. The issue that remained below the surface in both the discussion of charter schools and the common enrollment plan was the history of race and racism in Oakland as connected to both charter schools and district-run public schools. The distrust engendered by this history meant that it was difficult at board and community meetings to honestly debate Wilson's proposals. Anger at Wilson for these plans and for the failed ISS initiative led the NAACP to defend him against what they perceived as racist language during board meetings. As with the long-standing budget issues, collaborative, generative community solutions were blocked by distrust that came not only from Wilson's individual actions but also from a persistent history of race relations and racism.

The appointment of an insider, Kyla Trammel-Johnson, to run the district could be a tangible step forward. However, this move may not be sufficient for this district to turn the corner. Instead, drawing on insights gleaned from a close examination of Oakland, I argue that administrators and the community alike must understand and address the roots of the underlying distrust that shapes the history and actions of this school district and others like it.

Over the past eighteen years, neither local nor outside superintendents have had success in implementing new reforms in Oakland. Too often, people identify relational distrust or animosity toward individuals—whether they are local or outsiders—as the core of the distrust, rather than recognizing that it is rooted in history and politics. This historical account illustrates that the failure of school reform movements to recognize that relational distrust, necessary as it is to defuse, cannot successfully be addressed without addressing its roots. People *and* history matter.

3

Structural Distrust, Appointed School Boards, and Democracy

It was nearly 6 p.m. and the small boardroom was already overflowing with people; there were reports that more busloads of families would arrive shortly. Reporters vied with parents and politicians for seats, or at least a place to stand against the walls. There was an air of excitement and confusion as everyone waited to see what would happen next.

As a member of the recently appointed three-person school board in this small city on the outskirts of Philadelphia, I huddled in a nearby conference room with the other school board members, the superintendent, and our attorney on loan from the state. The size of the crowd meant that it would be impossible to hold this meeting, which was about capping the number of students in charter schools, in the regular boardroom, and we weren't sure we had the time or logistics to relocate the meeting. One of the school board members, who had experience in the district, suggested that we meet in the high school auditorium. Within moments, the space was secured. Soon, the local police officers were directing the people to larger space.

My knowledge of the neighborhood was still shaky; I was new to the community and hadn't yet been to the high school in the evening. Hastily,

I wrote down the directions to the high school and asked where it would be safe to park. My colleagues assured me that the police officers would help me figure that out once I was close to the school.

Nearly an hour later, the auditorium, was filled with over 350 parents, children, community members (including several pastors who regularly attended the meetings), newspaper and TV reporters—this was the first time I had seen TV newscasters at one of our meetings—and a few politicians. Seated on the stage were the new school board, along with the superintendent, legal team, and key district level administrators.

The huge crowd and the presence of statewide representatives from pro-charter school groups signaled the seriousness of the discussion. Many parents and children had arrived on buses organized by the district's largest charter school, Chester Community Charter School (CCCS); many wore red T-shirts that declared in bold letters "I Am Pro Choice." People passed out buttons to sympathetic audience members with the same slogan. Hand-printed signs held by young children and angry adults proclaimed allegiance to one of the district's three charter schools. Several signs were directed toward the school board members: "Afraid of Competition?" "The Board Should Resign." The community activists who were present at nearly every board meeting were less well organized, though neither quieter nor less passionate. A few people chanted, "What does CAP stand for? Cruelty Against Parents." As I glanced out over the crowd, I noticed a new sign: "CAP is WHACK. Are you afraid?" The atmosphere was filled with energy and emotion. It felt almost festive, at least for the moment.

When most people seemed settled, the board chair, Marc Woolley, called the board meeting to order. He explained that we would devote this meeting to hearing from the community about the proposed resolution to cap the number of students in the district's charter schools at their current level of 2,573 students. He emphasized at the outset that the recently appointed board was neither against charter schools nor against the choice they offered to the parents of Chester. The problem was that the amount of money that the district was required by law to pay to the charter schools for each special education student was substantially higher than the district cost and, as a result, it drained too much money from the budget. More than half of the district's K–8 students attended charter schools, and the costs to the district would continue to rise dramatically each year if their numbers increased. The bottom line was that without capping the numbers of charter school students at their current level, there would not be enough money to educate the remaining students in its district-run public schools. Woolley concluded that it was the board's responsibility to ensure the stability of the district. His words were drowned out by a mix of applause and jeers.

* * *

The account of this meeting captures the structural distrust that I observed throughout my time as an appointed board member and provides the context for a discussion about how distrust is often located in the political and governing structures of districts and schools, emanating from the policies and reform proposals that are intended to bring about change and opportunity. Drawing on a complex story of trust and distrust, local communities and appointed school boards, charter and district-run public schools, this chapter examines how structural distrust undermined leadership despite the school board's well-intentioned efforts to build trust and effect lasting change in a high-poverty school district. From my vantage point as a school board member from 2007 to 2010, I use an analysis of our efforts as a governor-appointed board to illustrate the generation of both visible and invisible distrust by our actions as leaders, as well as the distrust we encountered as we attempted to make change.

Through an examination of our choice as board members to build relational trust—at least with one segment of the community—while failing to notice and understand the overarching impact of the structural distrust, I suggest the parallels in other school leadership roles across a range of contexts. I begin with a brief history of the school district told through two intertwined narratives of educational reform: the imposition of an appointed school board and the privatization of the district's schools through the growth of charter schools. The story of charter schools in Chester highlights the complexity of this account of structural distrust by showing how the community was not simply pitted against the appointed school board, but also internally divided in its support of the district-run public schools and its allegiance to charter schools as an alternative to public schools that were perceived as failing.[1]

I entered this scene as a university professor committed to preparing teachers for urban schools and addressing inequities in high-poverty urban school districts. When I was asked by the governor to serve on the school board of this district, I saw it as an important opportunity to put my beliefs into action and work toward opening up opportunities and changing conditions for learning for young people and families in a nearby high-poverty community. I brought knowledge of teaching and learning, an anthropologist's perspective on understanding structural inequality, and a commitment to listening and working closely with the community to identify how to work with them to improve their schools. I believed that my commitment to work with, rather than for, the community would overcome the visible distrust we encountered on our first day.

A HISTORY OF DISTRUST

Chester is a small, high-poverty city with approximately forty thousand residents, about twenty miles from Philadelphia. The Chester Upland School District covers an area of just five square miles. At the time of this meeting, the per capita income of the city was $13,521, with a median family income of $30,900. These numbers were significantly below both Pennsylvania and national averages. Approximately 10 percent of the residents had college degrees. In recent years, Chester had been plagued by an economic downturn due to the disappearance of its industrial and manufacturing base—including shipbuilding and the nearby Baldwin Locomotive Works—and a loss of about a third of its jobs. As a consequence, the once-thriving city lost its middle class. According to the American Community Survey data from 2006–2010, Chester had a 13.5 percent unemployment rate, compared with 7.9 percent nationwide.[2]

In the latter part of the twentieth century, Chester became and remains a majority African American city, with African Americans making up more than 70 percent of the city population and nearly 98 percent of the student body in the schools. The impoverished city and school district is located in the middle of a predominantly white suburban county. Chester has been dominated by a strong Republican political machine since 1875. Until 2008, when Barack Obama ran for president and there was a concerted effort to register residents as Democrats for the state primary, the majority of the city's residents were registered as Republican and the city was governed by a Republican mayor. In a county and city where Republican Party politics determined who was hired and provided with services, fear and the promise of patronage kept the majority of the residents tied to the party in power.

Because of its dire financial circumstances and abysmally low test scores, for the greater part of two decades, the Chester Upland School District was overseen by governor-appointed school boards according to state statutes, which changed over time, identifying different purposes for the various boards, such as fiscal solvency and academic progress. In addition, the political party governing the state has changed every eight years, which meant that the educational strategies to address the struggling schools also changed, without significant advances in the quality of the schools or changes in the status of the district. During the time the district was run by appointed boards, a Republican-controlled elected board with limited powers also met. This dual governance meant that who represented the community—the appointed board, the elected board, or the activists who attended every meeting—was contested. Ultimately, it was the distrust that permeated the system that impeded reform efforts and empowered a tightly connected network of power brokers in the district, the county, and the state.

A controversial education reform strategy in the United States during the 1980s was the imposition of state-appointed boards to manage local schools in order to address the severe financial distress, particularly in urban areas. This reform reflected a broader trend away from local control of school districts and toward increased state oversight and control. State officials generally contend that the purpose of taking over a district is to improve public education through an increase in accountability. There are several ways that state governments assume authority over local school districts: they operate only the fiscal affairs of the district, as happened in East St. Louis, Illinois; they grant authority over the district to an elected chief executive, such as a mayor, as was done in New York and Chicago; and they replace locally elected school boards with state-appointed ones, as was the case in Chester.

Chester was initially placed under state control in 1994, after the state declared that the district was in financial distress, stemming from the poor fiscal practices of the elected school board. The state anticipated that, under the newly appointed board, the district would turn around in two years. However, its fiscal distress continued, as did its poor academic performance as measured by state tests, and the governor-appointed school boards remained in place.

Before the appointment of the Democratic board of which I was a member, the school board (called the Control Board) appointed by Republican governors turned to charter schools as a means to improve the district schools' academic performance. The largest of the three charter schools, Chester Community Charter School (CCCS), operated by a for-profit management company, opened in 1998 with fewer than one hundred students, using several rooms of a Howard Johnson motel for its classrooms. Soon after the charter school opened, the appointed board previous to the one I was serving on shuttered several district-run public schools on the west side of the city because of the declining school age population, while simultaneously allowing charter operators to open new buildings in the same geographic area. In the next few years, CCCS rapidly grew to more than twenty-six hundred students on two new campuses that each included an elementary and a middle school.

A cadre of engaged and vocal community members consistently opposed the proposed policies of the governor-appointed boards. This loose-knit group included long-time community organizers, a few activist pastors, engaged residents who saw the district-run public schools as key to the revival of Chester, retired teachers, and current parents. They vociferously objected to the policies that increased the number of charter schools, arguing for the need to preserve the public school system that had educated their families and relatives for generations. Distrusting the motives of the last appointed board's members, as they explained to us in our interviews, some community members assumed that their reason for turning to charter schools was the opportunity for a group of people—possibly the board members themselves—to make money from the education of their children.

As the number of families in the district sending their children to charter schools increased, the community became more divided, with proponents of the charter schools taking on a smaller and quieter role during board meetings. The pro–charter school parents generally attended only meetings that directly addressed the charter school issues—and then only when CCCS urged them to attend. There was little acrimony between the two groups as individuals; the hostility was aimed at the board members and the idea of charter schools as detracting from the district-run public schools.

In 2007, through complex legal maneuvers, Democratic Governor Ed Rendell dissolved the state oversight board and appointed what was called the Education Empowerment Board. This move was allowed under the Education Empowerment Act approved by Republican Governor Tom Ridge in 2000, which contained a provision for governor-appointed school boards in districts labeled by the state as "low-achieving." The board was composed of three Democrats, of which I was a member. During our two-and-a-half-year tenure, the elected board composed of Republican community members continued to meet periodically, and their chair sat with us during our scheduled meetings. According to the state legislation, the elected board's purview was limited to the oversight of severe discipline hearings and the approval of bond measures. As the new Empowerment Board, we immediately attempted to build trust with the community, including the elected board, while also assuring both groups that our time as board members was limited and we would soon hand the district back to them.

OUR ENTRANCE INTO THE COMMUNITY

Although over the past few decades, the distict's appointed boards had been primarily made up of white men, the Educational Empowerment Board comprised two African American males in addition to myself, a white female. Our chair, Marc Woolley, was an attorney with close political ties to the governor. He had worked for several public agencies, including the local port authority and the city housing agency. His law partner had been on an earlier board, and when Woolley indicated his interest in serving this district, Governor Rendell appointed him as chair. The secretary/treasurer, Juan Baughn, had been a high school teacher and well-loved basketball coach at Chester High School and had served as an interim superintendent in the district and the superintendent during the first few years that Edison, a private for-profit school management company, controlled most of the district schools.[3] Baughn worked closely with the state secretary of education to implement the secretary's vision of standards-based curriculum reform.

Although he had lived in Chester for a short period, during his tenure on the board, he—like the rest of us—lived outside of the district. I took on the role as vice chair. Before that time, I had been a teacher and principal in Philadelphia, and was now a professor at the University of Pennsylvania.

We were selected by the governor and his staff because of our range of financial skills and knowledge of high-poverty urban schools. These qualifications, however, initially meant little to the community, who were primarily concerned that we were outsiders with an assumed loyalty to the governor rather than to them. (In fact, people often commented about Juan Baughn that he had been in and out of the district for years and that they never knew when he would show up again—or leave.) From the beginning, we worked hard to develop credibility with the most engaged community members who attended board meetings, meeting with them individually and in groups. All the same, because we had been appointed rather than elected and were not currently residents of Chester, distrust was woven into our daily interactions with the community.

Our first board meeting illustrates the mixed reception we received from the engaged community members who steadfastly supported the district-run public schools. Even though for the most part we received a warm welcome, including positive and welcoming comments, there was also bitterness that yet another appointed board was running their district. Several people were angry that there were no community members on the board, calling this decision shameful and demanding that it should be remedied immediately. Their anger over our outsider status and their distrust of a state-imposed board trumped the fact that, in general, we shared their priorities and vision for the district.

Toward the end of the meeting, the comment of one community activist—a pastor—silenced the room, capturing the distrust in stark terms. This older African American woman shook with anger as she declared, "You are plantation owners." She went on to say that we should not be allowed to dictate the policies of the district, claiming that at least one of us should step down from the board to make room for a resident who could speak for the community. Her response to our decision to retain the board appointed by the governor emphasized the reciprocal nature of the distrust at work in the district: "You want us to trust people who don't trust us." She continued,

"Outsiders come in and they let us down . . . We have to sit on this end and watch you all make decisions about us . . . We understand Chester better than any of you." In the ensuing months, when we proposed new programs and new configurations of the schools, her refrain was, "You're making decisions for this community, and in five years, *we* are going to have to live with those decisions." It was hard to disagree with this assessment; although we had a deep interest in changing the educational opportunities in this district, our commitment was time bound and our knowledge limited by our outsider status.

ALIGNING OURSELVES WITH ONE SECTOR OF THE COMMUNITY

Charter schools were the source of the most charged discussions and difficult negotiations during our time as board members. I did not start off as a charter schools detractor. In the early 1990s, when the first charter schools were established, along with other types of school-based management, I saw them as sites for experimentation and models of what was possible with fewer bureaucratic encumbrances. As charters became a critical component of the education reform movement that embraces privatization, my stance changed. It was clear that Chester—like several other urban areas, including Oakland, who have a large number of charter schools—had reached a tipping point where the growing number of charter schools took too much money from the district budget, making it impossible to adequately fund the district-run public schools. The adverse financial impact of charter schools in Pennsylvania, as one example, was a direct result of the funding formula mandated by the state legislature, who were largely indifferent to those impacts. There was also little evidence, in Chester and across the United States, that charter schools were more successful in improving student outcomes than district-run public schools.[4]

In Chester, the most active parents, teachers, and community members who chose to engage with us were both the most demanding and the most responsive to our invitations to participate in meetings. They and we saw the charter schools as a threat to the survival of the district-run public schools. Although we knew that our decision to align ourselves with the sector of the community in favor of holding the charters at their current level meant that we were only working with one sector of the community, it was a decision driven by our understanding of the fiscal realities facing the district.

LEAVING THE DISTRICT: TRANSPARENCY AND STRUCTURAL DISTRUST

Throughout our tenure, in order to increase transparency, our board shared as much information as possible with the community at our regular meetings and in additional meetings across the city. Specifically, the superintendent went through the budget in detail by delivering long PowerPoint presentations and held forums across the community to explain the budget and the rationale behind various expenditures. Such meetings had never taken place before in the district. We also had regular meetings with members of the governor's team to explore innovative ways to increase the district's revenue in order to address the continuing structural deficit that we had inherited.

After our first few meetings, we rarely talked about the elected board's role in governing the district and consulting with us about decisions. We operated within a structural hierarchy that gave us access to the governor and state secretary of education without acknowledging the potential harm that accrued from these relationships along with their obvious value. Because of our relationship with the governor and secretary of education and their staffs, we were given access to resources that helped us to make changes in the district in line with what we believed to be the interests of the community.

In 2010, just as we had begun to convene a group of people to assess the progress of our board and think through the qualities the community desired in a new superintendent, the state legislature decided not to renew the Education Empowerment Act. This ended our tenure, giving control of the district back to the elected board after sixteen years. We anticipated that we would work closely with the elected board during the transition, as we wanted to insure our progress would continue. We were eager to work with them ahead of the date they officially took over the district to bolster their success and offered to continue working with them into the initial months of their term. We had several projects that were not yet finalized, and we wanted to make sure that they had enough information to follow through with the ideas. In addition, we knew that they had little knowledge of budgets and finance, and we were willing to work to bring them up to speed on the technicalities of reading and managing budgets.

Initially, the elected board welcomed our offers, and we set up a series of meetings to talk through the projects we were in the midst of funding and our new ideas for funding sources, such as a plan to collect delinquent taxes. In particular, we had a proposed bond measure to fund renovations of the former middle school where we had started a new small science-themed high school. However, the elected board did not show up for the first few meetings that we scheduled, and it quickly became apparent that they wanted to distance themselves from us. We assumed that although they had initially thought the meetings would be useful, they had been instructed by local Republican politicians not to interact with us.

Before the final meeting of the Education Empowerment Board, the elected board served us with an injunction to stop the bond issue to fund the new small high school. We stopped work on the bond, which was revenue-neutral, but asked the community to hold the new board accountable for their actions. In my closing remarks to the community, I said, "We didn't have enough time to accomplish everything we wanted to do, but we did begin to offer new opportunities, and that's what the bond deal represents. As we leave, we're handing the fight back to you." I then thanked the community for all we learned from and with them. We had worked hard to build trust, at least with the sector of the community who attended the board meetings. All the same, the community continued to exhibit a persistent distrust in us as outsiders and interlopers. We were leaving the district in a better financial and academic position than it had been in before our arrival. The question would be whether that position would hold. The role of trust and distrust in our accomplishments and in their durability was key, and one we would only understand after we left the district.

We had accomplished a great deal during our few years as a board. We made significant progress with the budget and deficit during those years. We held the number of students going to charter schools stable—and in the final year, they decreased—which was critical for the fiscal health of the district; we realized this goal by improving the district-run public schools enough that students began to return to those schools. We closed one charter school and turned it into a public school and initiated three new small public schools, reopening a building that was geographically and historically important to the community. We formed a partnership with a community group with private funding to open a public school focused on the arts (the group had originally applied to the district as a charter school). We opened fifteen preschool programs, including one located at a charter school, built playgrounds at every district-run elementary school, and supported the creation of several libraries. We hired new teachers for the first time in years and resolved a labor dispute that had forced teachers and support staff to work without a contract for the three years before our arrival. There were more honors classes and afterschool clubs at the high school. According to the traditional metrics, there were further signs of success. Graduation rates and test scores had slowly increased, and the level of violence decreased throughout the system. There was a level of stability, collaboration, and promise that had not been seen for years among the community, the board, the district including the superintendent, and school faculty and staff. These accomplishments were built on, and in turn enhanced, the relational trust that we carefully cultivated, especially with the activists in the district who supported the district-run public schools.

Within a year of when the elected board took over, however, nearly every one of our accomplishments was dismantled. The only visible signs of our work were the playgrounds. The district could no longer afford the small schools. The number of students in charter schools increased again, continuing to drain the district's financial resources, and class sizes in the district-run public schools soared. In a single year, nearly 40 percent of the district-run public school teachers were laid off. Teaching conditions worsened, and nearly all of the curricular reforms were put on hold because of the lack of funding. It was notable that the resources we brought into the district disappeared once we left and once a new Republican governor took office. In other words, this was another area where we relied on relationships rather than creating structures for enduring solutions, such as long-term funding, even when we knew there would be an inevitable change in political leadership. By creating new smaller schools that were dependent on bond measures we did not have the authority or time to pass, for instance, we made promises to the youth and their families that we were unable to keep. The trust we had earned by listening and responding to their dreams was fleeting.

Defending their layoffs, the elected board claimed that we had rehired too many teachers and overspent the budget, increasing the deficit. As the district was driven further into debt, the media reported that the new governor had not allocated enough money to provide adequate funding for the district. The media also accurately reported that charter schools and the funding formula, especially the payments for students categorized as special education students, had led to the district's fiscal insolvency. We argued that we hadn't been given enough time for our reforms to take hold. The tenure of the Empowerment Board, which had the trust of a governor who was willing to add new resources to the district, was simply too short. But I believe, in retrospect, that the persistent structural distrust, tied to the political forces and the power arrangements, that we never acknowledged nor adequately addressed was an essential component of our failure.

* * *

It has now been over twenty years since the district was first taken over by the state in 1994. The elected board governed the district for less than two of those years (between 2010–2012). Few, if any, of the attempts at reform—by both appointed and elected boards—have been successful. Trust has been gained and lost. In the meantime, the number of children in the charter schools have grown, as have the number of charter schools in the district. There is still no evidence that the charter schools are doing a better job educating the students, but some parents continue to value them for the safe and clean environment they provide. For a short time period, the test scores in the charter schools were higher; subsequently, it was alleged that teachers and administrators at the CCCS, which currently educates over half of the students in the district, were systematically erasing wrong answers to raise the test scores. CCCS was asked to monitor itself to discover whether or not there had been malfeasance and, not surprisingly, found no wrongdoing. However, after new procedures established closer oversight by state officials, scores plummeted to levels comparable to the rest of the district, strongly suggesting that there had been some form of cheating. The parents of charter students continue to be satisfied with the schools as evidenced by their growing number of students. There seems to be less of a divide in the community now; it was recently reported that 40 percent of the CCCS families also have students in the district-run schools. The grandchild of one of the most vocal opponents to the charter schools attends the arts school that we had begun as a district-run public school and that became a small charter school after we left the district. The lines have been blurred between the two groups as parents make decisions about what it best for their children. The elected board continues to meet, with the limited powers described above, while a state-appointed overseer holds his own board meetings. The fate of the district remains uncertain. There are pockets of trust. Yet for the most part, as the district continues to be run by outsiders, structural distrust and inaction persist.

THE NEED TO DIRECTLY ADDRESS STRUCTURAL DISTRUST

I define structural distrust as distrust that emanates from hierarchical structures or policies that impose regulations on organizations from a top-down position. It is generally the result of a power imbalance, with more powerful people or groups imposing their beliefs or policies on less powerful individuals or groups. Often, structural distrust in educational contexts comes from control by outsiders rather than local control of schools and districts. As noted above, one source of the structural distrust in Chester was the hierarchy of appointed and elected school boards, and the control of the district's schools by outsiders. As I show below, another source was bound up in how decisions were made about charter schools. Despite our intentions to improve the schools, we were part of a system, perpetuated by the politicians and developed in response to a school system in crisis, that placed outsiders in charge of a district in a paternalistic relationship.

Our power in Chester came not only from our positions as board members who appointed the superintendent and had oversight of the district's budget and the priorities, but also from our relationship to the governor and state secretary of education. We were part of a hierarchy that was inaccessible to the community. Many community members believed that replacing the appointed board with an elected board would be more democratic. (Given the patronage system in Delaware County, where Chester is located, which was ruled by the Republican Party at that time, the legitimacy of the elected board was open to debate.[5]) The community members distrusted the structures that put us into power and kept us in a hierarchical position that seemed removed from their quotidian concerns.

What characterized our work, and that of many boards and leaders in a similar position, was our reluctance and ultimate failure to address the structural distrust that characterized our relationships with the community. Instead, we focused on building trust with individuals and working with them to improve the educational conditions in the district. Our decision not to find a way to include a community member on the board was our first serious mistake. We adhered to the governor's advisers' conclusions that there was no one in the community with the qualifications to sit on the board. Naively, we believed that our connections to the governor, our willingness to listen to the community and act on their behalf, and our expertise in budgeting and academic issues would enable us to make lasting changes and overcome the distrust of the community. In other words, we believed that developing relational trust with the community would help us to build the social and political capital we needed to address Chester's problems. But we did not understand the limits of that approach. Without the direct engagement with the structural distrust that circumscribed our ability to work with all of the community, we were unable to make enduring changes.

Too often, leaders—whether they are principals, department chairs, board members, or superintendents—focus their attention on building community or developing trust without directly acknowledging and addressing the distrust that may underpin the discord. When a leader wants to introduce a new policy into a school building, the first step is often to develop buy-in for the idea, rather than exploring why there may be skepticism or doubts about its efficacy or viability, including the history of failed reforms or broken commitments that may have preceded the new idea. Ignoring this history often short-circuits the proposal and there may be resistance before the idea has been tested.

Structural distrust is particularly insidious, as it lives in power and hierarchies that are often largely hidden. Teachers and community members may reject new proposals out of hand simply because of their underlying and unaddressed distrust of the power structures. For instance, when educators introduced the small schools movement, the reform was initially met with skepticism by many of the teachers who had been through several waves of reform that had made little material difference in their teaching conditions and the lives of their students. As a result, a cycle of distrust ensued, where the teachers distrusted the process, and reformers distrusted teachers, whose motivation was interpreted as rooted in politics and lacking good faith.

Although our efforts to build trust may have felt successful to us in the moment, they could not overcome the structural distrust of the institutions that gave us our power. We were determined to quickly bring visible success to the district and poured all of our energies into building relational trust and addressing the daily challenges. Given this focus, we missed the opportunity to address the deeper structural issues that might have resulted in lasting change.

STRUCTURAL AND CONTEXTUAL DISTRUST AS IMPEDIMENTS TO LOCAL REFORM

From our first days as appointed board members, we understood the difficulty and complexity of the situation we wanted to address. What we failed to fully understand and address was the role of both structural and contextual distrust in impeding the process of change. We were cautiously optimistic that with additional resources, our own experience and expertise, time to build good will, and hard work, we could make a difference in the opportunities for youth in the district. And despite the structural distrust inherent in our position as an appointed board, we developed enough relational trust to allow us to reach several short-term goals. However, because we did not pay attention to the structural and contextual distrust, these successes proved ephemeral.

It may have been impossible, given our position as outsiders and the inherent power imbalance of an appointed board, to address the structural distrust we faced. All the same, we failed to create a collaborative partnership with the elected board. To do that, we would have needed to acknowledge the longstanding structural antagonism between Democrats and Republicans in this district that threatened to overwhelm our work. In retrospect, if the Republican state senator had asked that the members of the elected board not work with us (which we believed was what happened), we could have found a way to work through that impasse rather than blaming the elected board for seeking to undermine our efforts. This reciprocal distrust was mutually reinforcing.

In the end, we learned that it was not enough to build trust with only one sector of the community. We built trust by listening carefully and then responding to their concerns and by establishing real and symbolic forms of transparency, offering them several ways to participate in our decision-making. Rather than addressing the structural challenges, in the end we operated too much in the moment putting out fires and attempting to move forward with concrete results rather than paying enough attention to how we got there.

Money was a complicating factor in this story. We tried to enact lasting changes, but most of our initiatives were tied to money we received from the governor. When the elected board came back into power, the community wanted to trust them and also wanted them to be trustworthy. However, the elected board was unable to address the severe financial situation of the district and they did not have the relationships, outside knowledge, or a governor's support. Importantly, they dismantled the participatory practices we had established, increasing the structural distrust.

CHARTER SCHOOLS AS A SOURCE OF COMMUNITY DISTRUST

As the Chester example makes clear, charter schools can be a lightning rod in a community—viewed by some as a panacea for failing schools, by others as usurping the limited funding that is available for education, drawing students away from district-run public schools and ultimately responsible for the failure of those schools. Missing from these conversations is a discussion of the dynamics of trust and distrust around these issues, including an open conversation about who makes decisions and the evidence that informs the decision-making process. Too often families make choices based on the needs of their own children and then those individual choices are translated into policy without an analysis of the broader consequences for the entire system.

The charter school issue made it difficult for us, as board members, to build trust across the entire community and to represent the interests of all of the families in Chester. This issue was further complicated because the largest charter school, Chester Community Charter School was a for-profit educational institution run by outsiders. This dynamic generated another form of structural distrust among the community members most aligned with the district-run public schools and those we worked most closely with to build a trusting a collaborative relationship. There were several reasons why it was easier to work these members of the community: their positions matched our own policies; nearly all of the participants at our board meetings were from this group; they were the vocal and activist community members who showed up at citywide meetings, worked with us to choose the new superintendent, and participated on the long-range strategic plan and curriculum committees. In the meantime, by giving most of our attention to and focusing on building trust with just one part of the community, we failed to notice that we were exacerbating a divide, and distrust, between this group and those that supported charter schools. This divide reflected a structural problem, exacerbating the structural distrust inherent in the circumstances.

CCCS continues to be a source of distrust for much of the community, especially as newspapers report the gross inequities in the funding formulas for special education students in charter schools, and there are statewide calls for fair funding for education across the state. The story of charter schools in the United States and the larger story of privatization as a lever for educational reform is in part about the structural distrust of private management companies—especially for-profit organizations—that run public educational institutions. Charter schools, especially when they are a growing proportion of a district, inject distrust into the system. In this case, the divide in the community further exacerbated the distrust.

THE ROLE OF CONTEXTUAL DISTRUST IN CHESTER

The three forms of distrust—relational, structural and contextual—are nearly always intertwined. At the same time that we failed to acknowledge the structural distrust in the district tied to our relationship to the governor and to our appointment as outsiders to the board—at least in part because we were at a loss about how to address it—we also did not acknowledge or completely understand the contextual nature of the distrust we encountered.

Contextual distrust reflects the particularities of the local dynamics, including its history, politics and racial dynamics. For instance, the Chester Upland Unified School District is a predominantly African American district, located in a community whose residents are mostly African American Republicans. Two-thirds of our Empowerment Board, the superintendent, and nearly every member of his staff, including the attorney and business manager, were African American. While political party membership is changing, the tight hold of the Republican Party on this county, district, and city meant that party politics and community residency trumped race, creating a barrier that was difficult for us to move beyond, despite the racial composition of our leadership team. This legacy of contextual distrust was reinforced by the history of predominantly white governor-appointed boards that preceded us.

All of our interactions with individuals and community groups, including their distrust of us, were shaped by the history, politics, and sociocultural characteristics of the city and district. The district had a long, and some would say intractable, history of decline along with a narrative of a vibrant past. It was important for us to hold both of these stories at the same time—the impossibility and possibility of change, the history of poverty and failure along with the pride of past successes. We tried to remember these histories as we listened and made decisions, but, among all the other factors I have traced, the distrust from the community was also rooted in their perception that we could never fully understand their history and the conditions of their lives, even those of us who shared their racial backgrounds. In chapter 4, I elaborate this concept of contextual distrust in the narrative about our professional development work with Palestinian principals.

Today, the three forms of distrust persist in Chester with the presence of a state-appointed receiver who oversees the district. There continue to be conversations about breaking up the district and distributing it among its neighboring, largely white districts, declaring bankruptcy, and turning all of its schools into charter schools, though these discussions often fail to acknowledge that it was the charter school funding formula itself that accelerated the district's financial distress. These same reform ideas and conflicts are repeated in underresourced districts across the country, yet the nuances are specific to the context of this district. Any group of people or individuals that does not take into account the structural distrust of appointed boards and the related contextual factors that are part of the fabric of cities risks failure. Large infusions of money—like Mark Zuckerberg's $100 million grant to Newark (discussed in chapter 6)—will not turn around districts for the long haul, if the reformers do not recognize and address the distrust in the community. As the Chester story illustrates, we worked on addressing relational distrust without acknowledging or attempting to address the pervasive structural and contextual distrust and accordingly our relationships lasted only as long as we remained in the district. Now I read about Chester in the newspaper and watch what happens from a distance.

WIDENING THE LENS OF STRUCTURAL DISTRUST

The deep distrust of state-imposed control boards in Chester was one manifestation of the years of externally imposed "reform" initiatives I discuss in more detail in chapter 5. Federal intervention in local education has been controversial since it began a half-century ago with the initial attempts to enforce the civil rights laws. It is no small irony that the distrust of the Chester community toward outsiders engaged in educational change efforts had among its roots fifty years' worth of federal efforts to ameliorate racial disparities in educational access and outcomes. There is similar distrust of reforms imposed by state officials. The Chester community desired to be a part of the reform process rather than subject to outsiders imposing reforms—or reformers—on them; the political and structural sources of distrust evident in Chester are mirrored across the nation and likely across the globe.

Structural distrust arises from public policies, institutional practices, and norms that create power imbalances. It is not enough to build trust and relationships with individuals or even small groups of people, although as the most visible form of distrust, relational distrust can be addressed more easily and often more quickly. The structures that promote distrust, however, generally cannot be changed in the moment. Often these structures are historically, politically, and socially embedded in the fabric of the community and the systems that support community life. In other cases, they are sanctioned by outside government entities that are difficult to shift.

But frequently, the distrust runs both ways, and simply identifying it and acknowledging its source can make a difference in subsequent interactions. For instance, we might have acknowledged that we distrusted parts of the community as much as they distrusted us and pointed to our assumptions or the root causes of that distrust. The phrase used by the community activist at our first board meeting—"You are plantation owners"—felt both harsh and true at the same time. It never left my consciousness as I worked in Chester, making me cognizant always of how I always had a choice whether to impose my will or work with others to create the conditions for their own success.

What does using a lens of structural distrust give us in the analysis of why education reform fails? In Chester, it was clear that building relational trust was an important step for us to take as board members, but it was not enough. We needed to find a way to build trust with the entire community rather than only with those who were aligned with our vision. Our mission was to be a school board that represented all of the children and families of Chester, yet we chose to focus on just one, albeit a vocal and engaged, sector. That doesn't mean that we needed to embrace charter schools as the requisite reform in Chester. Instead, it suggests that we should have found more ways to actively engage the interests and needs of the entire community, rather than accepting the divide and limiting our focus.

More importantly, the lens of structural distrust suggests that when the expiration of the empowerment legislation marked the end of our term, the change in who controlled the district was not enough to eliminate the distrust. When the elected board came back into power, they also ended up creating an atmosphere of structural distrust with the community. For instance, they implemented policies of limiting participation at board meetings that reinscribed the hierarchies that should have largely disappeared once a locally elected board took power. In addition, initially their allegiance was more to the Republican state senator who controlled the patronage system in the city than to the local community whose schools they oversaw. Local boards are not a sufficient solution to structural distrust unless they speak in concert with their communities and enact policies and practices that invite the community into the decision-making processes. Especially now that special interest groups have begun to direct large amounts of money toward local school board elections, it is essential to preserve the relationship of boards to their own communities.

Distrust often accompanies change. At the same time, many educational reforms and people charged with enacting the reforms engender distrust. For instance, as described in chapters 2 and 6, the effort led by an outsider superintendent in Oakland, and supported by several different groups committed to principles of equity and access, to bring all public schools—district-run and charter—into a single system was met with resistance and distrust in the community. When the administration released a single document that included enrollment information for both public and charter schools, community activists, including union members, saw the move by the superintendent and his allies as an effort to defund the district-run public schools and build support for charter schools. They focused on the benefits that would accrue to the charter schools and the harm to the district-run public schools who would lose students and the funding that followed them. They did not recognize that there might have been shared democratic values held by each group. There was little opportunity for discussion and learning.

As is all too common, the superintendent left for another district before the distrust could be identified and worked through in order for there to be a resolution that moved the district forward in a positive direction. The structural distrust in this situation arose from misunderstanding, and also from a superintendent who made proclamations without first listening to and attempting to understand the community. The relationships that the superintendent built with sympathetic members of the community were not enough to overcome the distrust. Instead, the distrust served to widen the divide and made change more difficult to enact.

Structural distrust is often present when a principal, sometimes backed by a school board, attempts to enact a new curriculum and set of pedagogical practices without anticipating the need for a majority of the faculty to buy into the change. It may be that the principal has sought approval from a few departments—for instance, English and History—in a school for introducing writing prompts as formative assessment and forgotten to work closely with other departments—Mathematics and Science—to design the reform, even though it might help them to enhance student learning. As a consequence, the principal might be surprised that the reform is embraced by some faculty and not others. A possible course of action would be for the administration to examine the sources of distrust and respond to its roots, instead of the current manifestations. Rather than addressing the generic resistance or distrust, it may be useful to develop more specific responses to particular groups of teachers. Although the resistance may appear as relational distrust—or strained relationships between teachers and administrators—the deeper causes and possible solutions might be found in analyzing power and decision-making across the school.

An analysis of structural distrust provides those who seek to enact educational change and reform with a lens for tracing power and hierarchical structures, allowing them to locate decisions and actions in local communities, even if the people promoting the reform do not initially agree with the community's positions and anticipated actions. Any response to structural distrust needs to include people on the ground—the students, families, teachers, and community members—in the solution. And each response needs to be long-term and rooted in the community. Each time someone proposes a solution or reform—whether that individual or group is a local, state, or federal policy maker—it is critical to ask who will implement the reform, under what conditions, and how the reform can be implemented locally, without an imbalance of power, so that it does not get mired in distrust.

While it is always important to build relational trust—a strategy that has been tied to successful reform—it is equally, and often more, important to identify and acknowledge the structural distrust that will always arise when there is hierarchy and a disparity in who holds power. It is also critical to ensure that there is adequate time for the reform to take hold. And as I show in the next chapter, this hierarchical structural distrust is all too often deeply connected to contextual distrust, or the historical relationships that persist over time.

4

Contextual Distrust, Professional Development, and Politics

The Lebanese American University in Beirut sits on top of a hill in the middle of a city that is a mix of the old and the new. The markers of a bustling, modern city are interspersed with visible and daily reminders of war. On the way to the campus where we led professional development workshops, we passed local food stands selling *mana'eesh* and other traditional foods, European-style bookstores and cafés filled with young people, familiar fast-food chain stores, and the occasional tank guarding a building or intersection. To an outsider in January 2010, Beirut felt relatively peaceful and safe. In recent years, however, with its neighbor Syria engaged in a long drawn-out and brutal civil war, the daily reminders of Beirut's fragility—including increasing numbers of refugees—are ever more present.

On the first day of our workshop with principals, we arrived an hour early to set up the chairs, locate the chart paper, and confer with the interpreters. It was a conventional university classroom. An assortment of wooden chairs with attached desks were arranged in neat rows facing the front of the room, and light streamed through windows in the back, which opened onto a patio.

As we surveyed the room, we worried about accomodating a group of seventy-four school principals in the space. Our typical arrangement—seats clustered in small groups or one big circle—was clearly not feasible, but we resisted leaving the chairs in rows because we wanted to signal to the principals that we valued their participation and hoped they would use this opportunity to talk together and learn from one another rather than simply have expert advice delivered to them. At last, we compromised by arranging the chairs in several nested semicircles that faced the front of the room, where there was a line of four chairs for the three leaders and an interpreter. There was little space to move around, and we anticipated that asking people to rearrange themselves into small discussion groups would be next to impossible. As we waited for the principals to arrive, we were nervously excited about the potential impact of our work.

Since 1948, the United Nations Relief and Works Agency for Palestine Refugees in the Near East (UNRWA) runs all of the schools for Palestinians throughout the Middle East, and administers the social service infrastructure in the camps. It had hired us, through an international NGO, to give this series of workshops for teachers, principals, and administrators. This was my third visit to Beirut that year with my colleagues, Thea Abu El-Haj and Judy Buchanan, to work with Palestinian educators. A year earlier, we had conducted our initial professional development sessions in Lebanon, which were primarily with teachers, although each group also included three or four principals and supervisors. Now we were working with the principals of all the Palestinian schools in Lebanon, which we calculated represented thirty-three thousand children.[1] This meant that our work had the potential to reach every teacher and ultimately every Palestinian student attending an UNRWA school in that country.

While we were thrilled at this opportunity, we were also somewhat intimidated by the prospect of working with the principals, who were, we had been told, a tough group and always resistant to new ideas (although we had also heard that the next group, the supervisors, would present an even greater challenge). As the governing organization for the camp's schools, UNRWA appoints and supervises the principals. However, at times the principals were openly skeptical of and even hostile toward the UNRWA leadership.

As principals of schools located in refugee camps, they were in a challenging position, operating in contexts of hopelessness and despair. While we had been able to win over and engage most of the teachers and the few supervisors and principals in our initial workshops, we knew this work with principals alone, including those who did not choose to be part of the work, would be particularly challenging.

I use a description of our two-day workshop to explore ideas of contextual distrust—distrust that arises from local, historical, social, political, and economic factors. The principals entered this workshop with skepticism about professional development as well as deep skepticism that, as Americans, we could teach them anything that would be useful in their difficult situations. Underneath this skepticism, which we might have encountered had we done the same workshop in the United States, was a pervasive feeling of distrust—of us as leaders and also of one another.

We anticipated their wariness and also that they might distrust us, and actively worked to build trust with them from the first moment they walked into the room. What we did not accurately anticipate was the depth and persistence of their distrust of one another, which was grounded in history and politics. The contextual distrust among groups or factions with which each of the principals were aligned was based on long-standing divisions in their communities along with their shared histories, mirroring the kind of historical distrust among racial or ethnic groups that we might have seen in an underresourced school system and contexts shaped by conflict in the United States or elsewhere in the world. Whereas in the United States, the contextual distrust might have typically reflected racial or socioeconomic dynamics, among the Palestinian principals in Lebanon, at this time in their history, the context was shaped by political fault lines.

This chapter explores how we attempted to introduce new educational ideas in spite of the distrust we encountered and offers reflections about how we might have approached this task differently. In doing so, it sheds light on professional development connected to educational change that is often based on generic practices that frequently do not account for the local context.

ENCOUNTERING DISTRUST AND BUILDING TRUST WITH PALESTINIAN PRINCIPALS

At the appointed time, the principals drifted into the classroom. It was clear that they were sorting themselves in some way as they entered and arranged themselves in the room. Most were men in their fifties and sixties. There were about twenty women. We enthusiastically greeted the prinipals we had met on our school visits and at our previous workshops. However, we didn't know most of the participants, and many seemed to avoid meeting our gaze, choosing seats as close to the perimeter of the group as possible. While we tried to break through the distance between them and us with our enthusiasm and direct greetings, our pleas for them to sit closer were in vain.

We began with formal introductions by the country director of the Norwegian Refugee Council, the NGO that sponsored our work, and our colleague Dean Brooks, who had invited us to Lebanon. Next, I welcomed the group, giving my initial greeting in Arabic—*sabah elkhayr*—and then switching to English. As I introduced the workshop, including our goals and desired outcomes, I spoke slowly, in short phrases, so the interpreter could translate. Following my opening remarks, Judy and Thea each introduced themselves. In response to Thea's introduction in Arabic, during which she explained that she is Palestinian and spent her adolescence in Beirut, the principals applauded. One of the older men told her, "We are very proud of you." He said he was proud that she hadn't forgotten her roots as a Palestinian and was working to improve the lives of her people. Later in the morning, as part of a workshop activity, he wrote her a poem.

Following the introductions, I outlined the underlying ideas for the two-day workshop, explaining that our work was grounded in several concepts: listening, building community, and collaboration. Our framework for thinking about teaching was to engage students in learning on the basis of their strengths and a belief in human capacity. Our goal for the workshop was to explore with them how to move away from the all-too-common approach to teaching, in which teachers talk and students listen, toward a practice of listening carefully to students in order to understand how to teach them.[2] Our active workshop was structured so that participants would practice listening to and learning from one another. I told the group that while we would introduce ideas and tools, we would also listen carefully to their ideas in order to make the workshop responsive to their needs and local conditions.

Next, I described the three principles of leadership and change that framed the workshop and our approach to professional development, which we knew differed from their typical experiences. First, change comes from listening closely to and respecting the views and experiences of a range of people, including teachers, parents, students, principals, supervisors, and other members of the school community; such listening generates the trust required for change. Second, there are challenges and difficult conditions everywhere; change comes from an understanding of and response to local conditions based on multiple sources of data. Finally, change does not happen in a single workshop; it requires ongoing work.

The first activity was designed to demonstrate our expectation that the principals would actively engage in our work together, and to build trust among them and between the group and ourselves. We asked each participant to write a poem about a particular time in their lives. We envisioned this as a way for all of us to get to know each other and to begin to build a community so that we could work closely together over the next two days. This was an activity that I had used successfully in similar workshops: in earlier workshops in Lebanon with teachers, and also Indonesia and the United States. I emphasized that we would begin by listening to and learning from one another.

The response was a collective groan. As principals, they seemed to expect to stay disengaged during professional development workshops. "Teachers teach, and we lead and tell people what to do," their looks and body language told us. A few openly complained that they needed more time and warning for this kind of activity, which seemed to fall outside of what they considered their professional roles and obligations. We persisted, explaining that we would provide scaffolding to make it easier to write their poems. "This is an activity you can do with your faculty to build community in your schools," I added. Most still projected a somewhat distanced and uninterested attitude, appearing skeptical of what we—or any professional development—might have to offer them, given their difficult circumstances. They were polite to us and to each other, and slightly disengaged. A few, especially those who had worked with us in previous workshops, did smile and nod to indicate their encouragement, but they did so carefully, avoiding letting anyone observe their expressions of support.

As models, we read aloud stanzas from three poems: two by Naomi Shihab Nye, a Palestinian poet, and one by Garrett Hongo, an American from Hawaii.[3] Nye's poem "The Words Underneath Words" begins:

My grandmother's hands recognize grapes,
the damp shine of a goat's new skin.
When I was sick they followed me,
I woke from the long fever to find them
covering my head like cool prayers.

Hongo's poem "What For" opens:

At six I lived for spells:
how a few Hawaiian words could call
up the rain, could hymn like the sea

Nye's poems provided familiar images that we hoped would spark memories connected to a specific time in the principals' lives. Hongo's poem offered them a frame with the repeating line "At [a particular age] I lived for . . . ," which they could adopt as they composed their own poems.

At least a few of the principals seemed to enjoy the poems, especially Nye's. They nodded in recognition of her images and appreciated that we had found poems written by a Palestinian. But others were still unyielding. The men in the back of the room began to smoke cigarettes, appearing even more defiant. There were other signs of resistance among the principals that we tried to ignore. Had we been able to read the participants' body language and observe who they aligned themselves with, we probably would have noticed the divides between the various factions in the room. Instead, we continued, focusing on the principals who were visibly willing to engage in the activity.

This differences in response felt familiar, similar to what we had encountered in United States when introducing similar activities to principals. There are always people who seem visibly engaged, and those who maintain skepticism. The task of the leader is to respond in the moment to these reactions. In a context where we only partially understood the history and politics—and the local politics were strongly held and enacted—we struggled more than usual to understand the dynamics of this group.

"What are events, places, and memories that you have of a specific time in your life? Poetry is most successful when you are able to describe something in a few words with images that hold larger meanings. What are images that capture a certain and possibly powerful moment for you?" I asked them.

Together we generated categories that they could use as prompts for their own ideas. Their first suggestions included "Memories of Israeli air raids." "Memories of our lost homeland." "Memories of people dying." We wrote down each of their ideas in English and our interpreter translated them into Arabic. We attempted to develop larger categories from these initial ideas to encourage the principals to generate more words and phrases. While most of the suggestions were connected to political events and stances, some people added additional images: "Memories of weddings. "Memories of climbing a tree to find a nest."

"Select at least one of these categories," I suggested, "and generate a list of specific images you are reminded of when you think about the category. Remember to be specific. Think about an important or memorable time in your life." Instead of writing lists, most of the principals immediately began writing poems, subverting our process yet following our intention. Nearly everyone was engaged, although a few principals remained in the back, smoking cigarettes.

We gave them more time than we had planned, waiting until every person had written at least a few lines before we called them back together. Ultimately, they all wrote poems, even those who at first seemed most resistant. They appeared to appreciate the chance to reflect and write, slowly letting go of some of the weight they carried into the workshop. Although we had been confident in our timing during our earlier work with Palestinian teachers in Lebanon, we felt hesitant with this group, unable to detect their rhythm.

Typically, in our workshops, we give all participants the opportunity to read their entire poem to the group; however, because this group was so large, we felt pressed for time, so we asked them to simply read their first line. We also gave them the option to pass, though only one person chose this option. Our goal was for each person to have the opportunity to speak and be heard in order to build trust between and among the group members and ourselves. We asked for a volunteer to begin, and one of the principals we had worked with in a previous workshop read the first line of his poem aloud. As we continued around the room, the third principal read his entire poem. Afterward, we gently reminded the group to only read a single line or stanza. A few people followed our directions, but first one person and then nearly everyone read their entire poem. Many of those who had read just one line insisted that we return to them, so they could read their entire poem as well. At that point, we gave up on our tight agenda. Building trust, following the rhythm of the group, seemed to be more important.

The principals' poems were passionate, filled with the suffering endured by their families, their people, and frequently themselves. Most were highly political and addressed their feelings of loss for Palestine. Although almost none of them had lived in Palestine themselves—their families had left in 1948—they wrote about Palestine as their home and about their desire to return. A few people described the keys to their houses in Palestine that their family still kept. They also wrote about their fears of unexploded bombs near their homes in Lebanon and of the constant circling of Israeli planes overhead. One poem was about a baby who was sick and nearly died; another was about a wedding. One poem described in great detail the author's adventure climbing a tree to retrieve a nest and the surprise of discovering a large snake. Each of the poems carried the sadness that threaded through our conversations about their lives as Palestinians living in Lebanon as refugees and displaced citizens. For a brief moment, they seemed to trust us as leaders and each other as Palestinians who shared a common identity and history of suffering, struggle, and joy. We paused, soaking in the moment of trust that often occurs when people have shared intimate ideas and words connected deeply to their lives.

This moment did not last. Although we opened the workshop by introducing poetry writing as a way to build relational trust, it was difficult to move from that poignant moment to the more academic content of the workshop, and we quickly learned that this process of promoting interpersonal or relational trust among the principals, and between the principals and ourselves, was not enough to overcome the strongly held contextual distrust embedded in the larger social context. In the following sections, I explore the Lebanese context we encountered and then show how it played out in the workshop. I conclude by giving examples of contextual distrust in the United States.

THE CONTEXT FOR DISTRUST EXPERIENCED BY PALESTINIANS IN LEBANON

Almost two-thirds of the Palestinians in Lebanon—between 260,000 and 280,000—live in twelve refugee camps and their surrounding communities, which they call *gatherings*, established in the 1950s.[4] Originally established as tent camps, they now have more permanent buildings. Although these resemble the apartment buildings on the streets outside of the camps, they are more poorly constructed or maintained. Inside the camps, we often saw electrical wires illegally strung between crumbling buildings covered by graffiti and posters, reflecting their temporary nature. The schools run by UNRWA for Palestinian children and youth are located inside the camps.

The instability of the refugee communities and its impact on the nature of distrust among their residents cannot be overstated. For decades, Palestinian families in Lebanon have lived with constant fear, which translates into the school setting as a pervasive sense of precariousness and insecurity, and a frequent and overwhelming feeling that education is essentially useless. Competing political factions and parties also shape the experiences of students, teachers, staff, and principals. In 2009 and again in 2010, when we walked through the camps and observed some of the classes at a school, we could sense the fragility of students' home and school communities. At the same time, as outsiders, we could not truly understand the distrust that this precarity engendered. In response to what we saw and experienced, we developed a series of workshops that sought to build trust and learning among the principals, yet it turned out that the trust we sought to build was not sufficient to address the distrust that ran deeply through the communities.

Since the arrival of Palestinians in the 1950s, there have been ongoing tensions and distrust between the Lebanese and Palestinian populations. The debate about the precarious status of Palestinians as non-citizens has changed little since their arrival. When Palestinians arrived in Lebanon, the Lebanese were fearful that granting them citizenship and voting rights would lead to permanent settlements that would, in turn, disrupt the delicate balance of power (especially between Sunni Muslims and the dominant Maronite Christians) in the country's confessional government (a system that apportions political representation and resources by ethnic or religious sect).[5] For their part, the Palestinians feared that permanent settlement in Lebanon would be tantamount to giving up their right of return to their homes in Palestine; they believed exchanging refugee status for the security of citizenship would diminish the urgency of this goal. As one teacher told us, "We teach for the right of return."

Over the years, Palestinians have nonetheless sought to secure social and economic rights in Lebanon, but their appeals have been rejected. Along with the denial of their right to vote, Palestinians cannot own land or work in most professions. In recent years, many Palestinian schools have experienced high dropout rates, as youth see their opportunities to join the labor force diminished. These circumstances mean that most Palestinians in Lebanon live and work, when they do work, under a system that makes them dependent on local and international NGOs such as UNRWA, which in turn heightens their sense of powerlessness and distrust.[6]

DISTRUST INSIDE THE PALESTINIAN REFUGEE CAMPS

Most of the camps in Lebanon were physically separated from the surrounding urban and rural areas, essentially functioning as isolated enclaves. This separation shapes the quality of life within the camps and the mobility of their residents. In contrast to Syria and Jordan, where open camps afford easy access to the surrounding communities and living conditions are similar to conditions outside of them, the camps in Lebanon are cut off from their surrounding communities, fenced in by walls and barbed wire, and monitored by security guards who restrict access at entry points.[7]

In recent years, the Palestinian camps in Lebanon have housed competing political factions. In some, there are more than fifteen political parties, each controlling different geographic areas. These factions are reinscribed in schools, where not only students and families, but also teachers and administrators, hold competing allegiances. The 1969 Cairo Agreement between Lebanon and the Palestinian Liberation Organization (PLO) gave the PLO power to govern the camps through popular committees. At the time, the PLO was the political structure for the various political parties, militarized groups, and social institutions in the camps. During this time, the Lebanese police were not allowed to enter camps without negotiating with the popular committees. In 1982, the Lebanese government forced the PLO to leave the country, and dismantled the PLO popular and security committees, replacing them with committees who were perceived as weaker and pro-Syrian. Rather than recognizing these new committees, residents went to *imams* and local leaders to resolve disagreements before going to the police.

By the time we visited Lebanon, there was a growing crisis of governance in the camps. Although the many different political factions—including multiple groups affiliated with the PLO, pro-Syrian groups, and Islamic militant groups—attempted to work together in coalitions, as well as with UNRWA, these coalitions often fell apart, leaving a sense of imminent if not actual chaos.[8]

We visited several camps in both the north and south of Lebanon to learn about the schools and their surrounding communities. At their gates, we were often held up for long periods, sometimes hours. If one of our names had been misspelled or the information from our passports or permission forms had been inaccurately transmitted, the security guards would check and recheck the information. We were not the only ones waiting, but the camp residents who accompanied us seemed accustomed to this level of inconvenience, scrutiny, and other outward signs of structural distrust. Because we worked with all of the teachers in one of the schools in a large camp in the south, we were able to visit that camp on two separate occasions. Our experience there gave us a deeper understanding of the contextual distrust we experienced later in our workshop, though we didn't fully realize the connections until later.

We were told that the densely populated camp we visited in the south was violent, though we were assured of our safety on the day of our visit. The camp had more health centers, schools, and NGOs than many others. Its streets were crowded, noisy, and quite narrow. When the driver attempted to park our van at the local hospital, he was told he would need to move it because the hospital was actually a military base.

Like the camp itself, the schools felt crowded and noisy. The elementary school principal told us that when students walked to school, they passed through several areas controlled by different factions. Much of the all-too-prevalent playground violence came from children acting out the animosity between the factions. The boys' secondary school that we visited was known as the most violent school in the camp. When there were outbursts of extreme violence in the schools, they closed the school and sent the students home. We were informed that nearly every adolescent and adult male had a gun and that indiscriminate shooting was common—on occasions of both anger and celebration. Students sometimes brought guns to school.

Exposed to military hardware and guns on a daily basis, the children and youth had a high threshold of acceptance of violence not only externally (from the conflicts among the factions) but internally (from their families). Many parents believed that physical violence was the best form of punishment, though we also witnessed physical affection, closeness, and loyalty among family members as we walked through the camps. Parents held kids in warm embraces one minute and hit them when they disobeyed, the next. Where verbal violence and insults led to escalations in conflict, the parents believed, physical violence insured that the youth learned the necessary lessons for their survival.

This attitude was evident in the schools. A cause of the principals' unhappiness with UNRWA was the elimination of corporal punishment as part of what UNRWA called the "safe schools, happy schools" program to reduce school violence. Both principals and parents believed this policy was a Western conspiracy to prevent their children from learning. They thought that without corporal punishment, teachers and principals would no longer have the same the authority as the parents and, as a consequence, the children would feel as though they could verbally, or even physically, abuse the teachers. The principals often referred to this as the "new code of conduct," and, from their vantage point, it limited their authority with both parents and students.

The camp we visited in the south had between seven thousand and eight thousand school-age youth, nine elementary schools, and a single secondary school with separate sections for boys and girls. When all of the teachers were in school, a typical class size was forty-five students. When a teacher was absent, classes were combined and there could be sixty students per class. As students reached higher grades, many dropped out (with their parents' approval), and class size decreased. For many of the teachers we spoke with, the youth represented hope, and they believed that teaching was a positive contribution toward building the future. However, the students displayed an acute sense of hopelessness, fueled by a belief that education was essentially immaterial for their future life chances. We often saw students wandering in the halls during class times, with no apparent consequences.

The reemergence of community tensions in schools is a pervasive dynamic in the camps, as it is in educational institutions around the world. The Palestinian teachers and school leaders felt compelled to address these tensions as they manifested in their school settings, although often to little avail. Educational institutions are never entirely separate from their surrounding contexts. As a result, the distrust that emanates from community contexts shapes the possibilities for change in schools, as it did for us with the Palestinian principals.

PROFESSIONAL DEVELOPMENT IN A CONTEXT OF CONFLICT AND CHANGE

A significant, and often overlooked, aspect of educational reform is the critical role principals and teachers play in enacting reform ideas in their schools and classrooms. When reforms are mandated without the opportunity to adapt them to local contexts or for teachers or principals to learn how to do the work, they often run into difficulties. One explanation for the failure of several waves of reform, as I discuss in chapter 5, is that teachers were told to teach differently than how they learned as children, without sufficient professional development opportunities to learn how to do so. A prime example of this is the New Math curriculum that curriculum leaders across the United States introduced in the post-*Sputnik* era. This reform failed after a short time, in part because there was little effort to introduce this new and more conceptual way to teach mathematics to teachers and parents through extended professional development. Recent critics of the implementation of the Common Core Standards have made similar arguments. Too often, professional development workshops are mandated and led by "experts" rather than practitioners who may have more knowledge of current classroom contexts (I return to this idea in chapter 6).

Following a pattern that is common in the United States and much of the world, nearly all of the professional development programs offered to the principals and teachers in the UNRWA schools follow the stand-and-deliver format. Experts stand in front of the room and explain new strategies, which the principals or teachers choose to either take up or reject once they return to their schools. The ideas, tied to specific educational reform agendas, are often generic and assumed to be useful, or "best practices," for every context and every school.

We chose a different tactic. Our goal was to introduce a conception of teaching based on knowing students and their strengths and interests as a way to engage youth in school. In other words, we took an asset-based approach (discussed in chapters 5 and 6). This approach was connected to the recent UNRWA agenda to make schools more humane and learner-centered. Rather than giving the principals answers or formulaic methods for teaching, we gave them a set of principles to guide their practice and asked them to participate in the workshops as learners. In addition, our focus was to teach a set of protocols that they could use to draw on the knowledge and strengths of their teachers to shift the teaching practices in their schools. We taught and then enacted these protocols in the workshop so that the principals could experience them and think about how to adapt them to their own contexts.

A Dilemma of Practice: The Impact of Contextual Distrust on Principals' Work Together

Although the principals were initially reluctant to participate in the poetry-writing activity, when we asked them to read their own poems aloud, their stance shifted. They moved their chairs a little closer together, signaling both their interest in hearing their colleagues' poems and a modicum of support for our work together. They laughed and sighed and often seemed deeply moved by words and descriptions that rang true. They shed their political differences, uniting around a common identity as Palestinians in a hostile world. For a brief moment, it seemed as though we all pulled closer together.

After the poetry, we did several activities that introduced and then elaborated on the idea of collaborative mentoring as a process to improve teaching practice. The principals were moderately engaged, especially during the demonstrations that they watched rather than actively participated in. Just before lunch, we asked the principals to submit questions about challenges in their schools that we would address through a protocol we call "dilemmas of practice," which is based on a descriptive inquiry process developed by Patricia Carini and her colleagues from the Prospect School and Center for Education and Research.[9] We explained that we would select three questions and then, after lunch, divide them into smaller groups so that we could teach them the protocol to use with their faculty. Over lunch, we chose questions from principals we already knew or felt confident could present to the group. We also looked for questions that seemed compatible with the type of conversation we planned to lead.

When we reconvened, we attempted to divide the group so that the clusters of principals who had segregated themselves into exclusive groups, and especially the resistant male principals who sat in the back, would be spread evenly across three groups. However, the principals reorganized themselves into their chosen clusters. As a consequence, the group I led was relatively large and had most of the difficult older male principals, including the most skeptical. My group remained in the large room while the other two groups went to nearby smaller rooms.

The question for our group, presented by a high school principal named Mohammed, was, "How can I manage the senior boys so that they attend their classes?" To begin, we asked Mohammed to state his question and describe its context. Next, there was a time for clarifying questions to help the group formulate recommendations. Finally, the group made recommendations while Mohammed listened without responding. We attempted to limit each of these segments to ten minutes to show that the entire discussion could fit into a typical staff meeting. As the chair, my role was to keep the discussion focused by summarizing the major themes after each round, fielding questions and comments, and reminding participants of the task and purpose of the activity.

In establishing the context for his question, Mohammed explained that the boys who frequently skipped classes were in the Economics track—the lowest track of his school. This meant that their national test scores were among the lowest in the school and their employment prospects for anything more than menial jobs were dim. The boys did not attend classes they perceived to be unimportant for graduation, including English and history. During those classes, they lingered in the hallways and disrupted the other students and teachers.

Despite my best efforts at facilitation, after Mohammed described the problem, the question period quickly veered away from a focus on the students to a focus on the teachers and administrators. The principals asked a wide range of questions, some informational, others confrontational. One asked, "What strategies have you used?" Mohammed replied that he had called parents individually and invited them to meetings, and he had worked with teachers to change their approaches. Another principal inquired, "Honestly, is there real cooperation between you and the teachers? Are they convinced that you are a good principal?" Mohammed admitted that some teachers were not working 100 percent and that he had difficult relations with them. "Did you take severe punitive measures?" another person queried. "Some students belong to various factions and they are students at the same time. Have you met with the leaders [of their political factions]?" "Do the teachers who don't cooperate belong to the same political faction?" "Does the political faction supporting students not to attend their classes support you?" Mohammed stumbled through his responses. I felt increasingly uncomfortable with the mounting tension, yet I had few resources to defuse it aside from encouraging them to adhere as much as possible to the process we had introduced.

It soon became apparent that Mohammed and the administrators he had appointed were members of one political faction (which I later learned was a "weak" political party in this camp) and the resistant boys were predominantly members of another political faction (the "strong" political party). Mohammed explained that the administrators and teachers were divided between people who belonged to the boys' political faction, and who had apparently told the youth it was acceptable for them not to go to classes, and people who belonged to the Mohammed's faction, who wanted the behavior to change. As a result of these conflicting messages, Mohammed felt he had no recourse, and the boys were allowed to roam the halls at will. His question, "What can I do about this situation?" thus went well beyond the typical question that teachers and principals ask when students skip classes: "How can we engage students so that they will attend their classes?"

The problem-solving process we introduced is meant to proceed in an orderly manner, with one person speaking at a time. When it goes according to plan, people ask questions and make recommendations without directly debating one another. The idea is for the discussion to remain focused on the presenter's dilemma rather than the disagreements between the participants. The questions and recommendations are typically directed to the presenter and meant to clarify and then respond to his focusing question, which is helpful for keeping the discussion on track.

However, because of the factional divisions, when a principal would make a forceful statement that indicated his political allegiance, others would immediately interrupt and contradict him, offering counterstatements with equal intensity. The contextual distrust in the room was played out in the verbal interactions between the various participants.

When we moved to the recommendation portion of the protocol, the principals offered a wide range of suggestions to Mohammed, including constructive ones, such as giving the boys positive leadership opportunities and starting afterschool clubs for them. The first person who spoke said, "I know Mohammed. We all know we are all facing many problems and a lot of pressure. And a lot of interference. People are trying to make you fail. There are new rules limiting our actions. If someone is expelled, there is anger. The new code of conduct limits our authority." One person suggested that the teachers receive more training to meet the needs of the students. Another recommended that the principal conduct dilemma of practice sessions similar to this one with the parents, in order to address the absenteeism and the problem of students leaving the classroom. Someone suggested that Mohammed identify two or three of the strongest teachers to talk to the students.

Then one principal, backed by several others, interrupted the constructive discussion and stated boldly that Mohammed should leave his job because he had not acted decisively at the beginning of the year. Arguing that the problem was Mohammed's own political affiliation, he said that Mohammed should be more willing to work with all teachers and students equally. Another principal asserted that Mohammed should come down hard on these boys and issue a strong punishment even if it meant closing the school down for a month. The recommendation session rapidly devolved into an intense and heated discussion across political factions.

Throughout the discussion, Mohammed remained quiet. At the meeting's conclusion, a number of people said that they appreciated Mohammed's honesty and the fact that he had brought this problem to the group. One said, "Thank you for discussing a problem we all hide."

During this part of the workshop, I found it difficult to insist on the listening necessary to insure respect and trust in the group. I attempted to maintain a steady voice and presence, even though I worried that the process was disintegrating. As I worked to keep the discussion orderly, I felt as though I was actively staving off imminent physical fights. That night, as we reflected on the process, we realized that, as facilitators, it was naive of us to believe that in such a short period of time we could develop strong enough relational trust with this group that could carry them through this difficult conversation, given the daily vulnerability and distrust they experienced. The power dynamics among the group, which had previously been invisible to us, became more apparent. As the principals spoke, we began to understand the contextual distrust that pervaded the content and affective dimensions of the conversation.

Yet, at the conclusion of the day, the principals, and later the UNRWA director, told us that they had enjoyed the workshops and learned a tremendous amount. The UNRWA director added that it was the calmest workshop he had been in and cited the fact that there were no actual fistfights as evidence. If our activities hadn't achieved our goals during that first day, they had clearly succeeded in some ways. The principals indicated that they would use both the information and the formats we had introduced when they returned to their schools to inform their work, although given the brevity of our time together, it was impossible to confirm this.

That evening, we redesigned the next day's workshop to address the challenges we had experienced and our growing understanding of the contexts the principals brought into the room. Since they seemed to find value in the new processes that invited them to collaboratively develop solutions to their challenges, we wanted to give them more leadership in this work, as well as guidelines to keep the conversations more focused. Our goal was to make it more likely that they would continue this work beyond our time together. We developed a set of stricter guidelines for maintaining respect in discussions and thought carefully about how to design the next activities to account for the contextual distrust that threatened to derail the workshop. We considered what the principals might need to learn and experience to make them willing to enact our protocols in their schools, as well as how we might adapt the protocols according to our growing understanding of the local context. We also added a different kind of trust-building activity to start the day. I now understand that naming and addressing the sources of distrust was a critical step. We took a different approach toward creating conditions for them to work together, however, and asked them to work collaboratively with colleagues from nearby schools to map the resources they had in common in the local communities adjacent to their schools.

The next day, the mapping activity went well. In smaller groups that were still politically diverse but locally based, the principals listened to one another and collaboratively designed new activities built on shared resources. Rather than attempting to solve problems, they built new knowledge together and offered each other advice about issues that were not politically charged. At the conclusion of the workshop, many ranked this activity as their favorite part of our work together.

In the afternoon, we initiated another round of dilemma of practice sessions with three new groups and three new questions. The satellite rooms we had used the previous day were no longer available; with all three groups in the same room, it was crowded, noisy, and often difficult to hear. So that the principals could practice leading the protocol, in each group we asked one to present a dilemma and another to chair the session. This was our attempt to address structural or hierarchical distrust in the groups. We hoped this shift would defuse the previous day's tension and disruptions and also encourage the principals to take the process back to their own schools. One of us worked with each group as a coach to help them stay on track and to make the necessary adjustments, given the distrust we anticipated. I worked with the two female principals whose question was: "What can we do with 'careless girls'—those girls who throw away their ambitions to become rock stars who can quickly earn large sums of money?" Their question indicated their disappointment that their female students were failing to pursue realistic goals. Although the conversation had a few tricky moments, for the most part it went quite well, and the group offered an interesting and useful set of recommendations. The principals also listened to one another and withheld their criticisms, respecting the leadership of the chair.

My colleague Thea oversaw the group that included a large number of the contentious male principals. As they had the day before, they gave the presenter a difficult time because he was from a weaker political party. He was a principal from a small school, and his question was about how to help a "weak" teacher. After a short time, several of the principals began arguing with him and suggested that he quit his position. Thea made the decision to stop the conversation and end the session before it got out of hand. The principal who had presented his dilemma later told Thea that he feared retribution, although he reassured us that he had expected to present a dilemma and was glad to receive the feedback. Though Thea had initially built relational trust with the principals through her identity as Palestinian, it was not enough to counteract the contextual distrust that the principals brought into the session.

At the end of the second and final day of the workshop, a principal and the head of the union asked if they could have five minutes to make an announcement. They informed the principals that some of the forms for claiming reimbursement from the UNRWA office needed to be revised and that they should not fill forms out until corrected ones were available. In response to this request, there was a heated exchange that we could not follow, although all of the principals seemed to be on the same side. In their common structural distrust of the bureaucracy, the contextual distrust among the various factions in the union appeared to lessen, at least for the moment, and perhaps a modicum of trust was built. The principals were united in opposition to the UNRWA authorities who oversaw their schools.

This brief moment provided us with a final insight into how we might have addressed the contextual distrust we faced. When we focused on finding commonalities and building relational trust—in the poetry writing and the collaborative mapping activity—the principals engaged in our work and with one another. In our desire to introduce the protocol for discussing dilemmas of practice, which in turn raised issues that were tied to political factions, we created a situation in which the contextual distrust overwhelmed the principals' desire to work together. Further, we introduced a process that had been successful in various contexts in the United States, without fully exploring the norms that would make it work in this particular locality.

If we had been more aware of the impact of factions, for instance, we might have collaboratively developed a set of questions for the group to address, rather than putting individuals and their questions onto the hot seat, which became more precarious as the session progressed. While we might have lost some of the details and local context that make conversation richer, we would have gained a protocol based on local practices that facilitated the conditions for trust and enabled a productive conversation. Further, we might have drawn on the knowledge of the group of principals to repair the distrust so that they might build collectively on the processes we had introduced to them.

REFLECTIONS ON BUILDING TRUST WITH PRINCIPALS IN A PRECARIOUS CLIMATE

The distrust we experienced in our work with the principals—both toward us and, more intensely, toward each other—was closely connected to their daily experiences as refugees living and working in difficult, often hostile, conditions. The multiple layers of their distrust included structural distrust of the UNRWA hierarchy, who mandated their attendance at this workshop, and relational distrust of us as Americans, who could not possibly grasp their daily realities. We attempted to build relational trust by listening carefully and paying close attention to the needs and desires of the group. Thea had an additional advantage as a Palestinian who speaks Arabic. The handful of principals we had worked with in previous workshops were more outwardly relaxed and open to us. The rest, while outwardly polite, mostly distanced themselves from us. Although we had spent a few days visiting the camps and particularly the schools, they knew that our understanding of the conditions for leading the schools was circumscribed by our status as outsiders.

Although the principals had all been teachers themselves, they seemed to be in more difficult and conflicted positions than their teachers. They had risen to their positions as administrators for a variety of reasons, including their political connections: their positions and locations in their community were often tied to one of the political factions or parties; they had been involved in politics as a way to obtain a more highly paid administrative position; and most continued to stay active in politics at a local level and through their union and various allegiances. They brought their political allegiances into their schools and to our work together. While the teachers in our workshops had been more optimistic about the possibilities for their students and interested in improving their teaching practice, the principals were in general more pessimistic about the future and more resistant to change. We could not know or fully understand their vulnerabilities or the ways that they needed to posture and present themselves to their peers in workshops such as ours.

This work with principals seemed both familiar to work I had done with teachers and principals over many years and also different, grounded in its own set up politics and contextual issues. The time limitations were familiar, including the difficulty of enacting deep and lasting change in a relatively short time and the challenge of translating across contexts. Working to read the interpersonal dynamics and political complexities in a country where I had only surface understanding of the history and current political dynamics was more challenging. Although the poetry and other activities broke down some barriers and forms of resistance, the work remained difficult. Reflecting back on this situation, it is clear that we did not understand the depth of their distrust across political factions. In retrospect, we might have been able to read the signals from how they grouped themselves for the various activities. Although we attempted to remain flexible and adapt our work with the group as we proceeded, the small changes we made were not sufficient to address the contextual distrust that arose from years of history and current political conflicts.

In addition, we did not have a clear enough understanding of the local context, and especially the role politics and history would play in the dynamics of the workshop. We designed a workshop that was flexible and responsive to the principals' needs and desires, following the format that was successful with the groups of teachers. We anticipated that by building trust at the outset of the workshop, we could create an atmosphere of collaboration and an openness to new ideas. Instead, we encountered a group who were most concerned with maintaining power and allegiances both within their schools and the larger community. This suggests the importance of recognizing and understanding the role of trust and distrust in professional development, including the necessity of identifying the distrust that often accompanies new ideas both in the design of workshops and in their enactment.

Ultimately, however, their contextual distrust overwhelmed our ability to create the lasting sense of trust that would have supported deeper, more enduring work. The political, social, economic, and historical context of the principals' work lives shaped their ability and willingness to work together in a collaborative setting. Most professional development is generic, and professional development providers often have little understanding of the local context, including the social and political conditions of the schools and their surrounding communities. As a result, many professional development programs are rejected by teachers and administrators and ultimately have little impact on teaching and educational change. When teachers or principals do not perceive that those leading professional development have a deep understanding and respect for their local contexts and the daily exigencies of their teaching, they are unlikely to believe the new ideas will be helpful. Qualitative researchers who focus on documenting the particularities of an educational experience understand and pay attention to the local context and its importance for teaching and learning. As Frederick Erickson explains, " . . . A teacher does not teach children in general, but particular children in particular circumstances of learning and teaching in classrooms and in community life."[10] This extends to professional development work with both teachers and principals. The necessity of understanding the local conditions for teaching and learning is intimately tied to professional development, especially in contexts characterized by conflict and distrust.

Contextual distrust is often built on past relationships, which may have deep-seated histories that extend beyond the temporal or spatial boundaries of educational institutions. People bring histories into their relationships and educational spaces. For principals and teachers, this history may be rooted in the community; it may arise from their political affiliations; it may be connected to racial and social class positions; it may be connected to deeply held beliefs and values; and it may be connected to particular events.

The contextual distrust we witnessed in Lebanon was distinctly local. It was born from particular local conditions and histories that shaped all of the interactions in our workshop. As noted, we had anticipated the participants' distrust toward us and sought to mitigate it by developing a workshop that included listening to and paying attention to their interests and desires. But once we realized the depth of the distrust, we might have more deeply integrated a listening stance into our activities, rather than largely following our original workshop design, so that our work together was even more responsive to their local conditions. Listening, in such instances, is much more than giving people an opportunity to talk. It involves being open to learning in each moment. Listening also involves being attentive to the local, historical, social, and political contexts and attuned to the interpersonal dynamics of the individuals involved in the process.

Ultimately, though, in order to plan a workshop that truly addressed the needs of the principals, as well as the teachers and supervisors we worked with on other visits, we needed to spend far more time in the schools and communities, to understand the local circumstances, which were specific to this country, the particular people we planned to work with, the specific camps, the set of schools, and the individuals in the classrooms and communities. And we needed to engage the principals themselves in the design of the workshop. The notion of teacher-led or collaboratively designed professional development is becoming more common in the United States. While it has not been part of the UNRWA education reform strategy for their schools, there is no reason we couldn't have tried the process and insisted on more time. It also would have been invaluable to insist on longer-term professional development that was more closely integrated into the local practices of the school sites, which would have more closely resembled the work we typically do in the United States.

WIDENING THE LENS OF CONTEXTUAL DISTRUST

The notion of contextual distrust is useful for understanding how the local context—including the sociocultural and political understandings and histories—can both shape and limit opportunities for teaching and learning and, ultimately, for educational change. Nearly every educational situation is shaped by its local context. When that context contributes to distrust, learning is compromised. Our work with the Palestinian principals in Lebanon provides a vivid account of contextual distrust. The precariousness and vulnerability of their lives increased the difficulty we had in building trust and addressing distrust between the members of the group and between the group and ourselves as leaders. In our activities together, we observed how the principals brought the distrust they experienced in their schools and communities into the workshop. This distrust made it difficult for the principals to learn new ways of interacting with one another and to collaborate to learn together.

If we had found ways to better understand the local context, and, importantly used that understanding to shape our professional development activities—from engaging participants in planning the workshop to redesigning protocols to meet local needs and expectations—we might have addressed the contextual distrust both directly and in our learning strategies, and in turn effected deeper, long-lasting change. As rapidly evolving local, regional, and international political events make it more difficult to understand the perspectives and histories of workshop participants at any moment in time, it is more critical than ever to do this kind of attentive, inclusive professional development work.

US educators who are working to enact change through professional development and other means often encounter contextual distrust similar to what we found in Lebanon. Such distrust is often present when people attempt to work together across racial, ethnic, linguistic, or socioeconomic differences, which might be analogous to the political factions in Lebanon. Although they tend to be invisible and remain unnamed and unaddressed, these tensions can disrupt work when groups need to collaborate in decision making, whether it is a professional development session, a staff meeting, or another kind of working group.

Contextual distrust is also present when groups of students and teachers who have formed separate identities or allegiance inhabit common spaces. For instance, several reforms bring youth from different neighborhoods together into a single school or building. Demographic shifts and the growth of charter schools have led to the closure of schools in Chicago, Chester, Oakland, and many other urban and rural communities across the country. Across the United States, a majority of school closures occur in high-poverty African American and Latinx neighborhoods, forcing students from different neighborhoods to attend school together. A similar disruption occurs when schools are reconstituted, which generally involves removing the administrators and at least 50 percent of the teachers and rebuilding the school with mostly new staff. When neighborhood schools are closed or teachers forced to leave, students and teachers are dispersed into new schools that may or may not be proximate to their communities, forcing some students to travel across the city to attend school. This same phenomenon occurs when districts introduce an open-enrollment policy that allows students to leave their community school and, if they have access to transportation, enroll in any school in the district. In addition, students from disparate communities also occupy the same building when schools populations shrink, making space for two or three separate schools to co-locate in a single building. While any of these arrangements may prove to be successful, there can be serious tensions or contextual distrust between the different groups of students and teachers in the new configurations.

In the best-case scenario, when youth from various neighborhoods come together in a school, they learn about each other and gain knowledge from the range of perspectives and experiences they bring to their education. But too often, particularly in urban neighborhoods that have experienced high levels of poverty and violence, students belong to disparate, often warring, groups—sometimes coalesced around gangs or factions. The contextual distrust caused by combining schools is similar to the distrust felt by the Palestinian principals. In this context, too, it often remains unaddressed. Teachers and administrators might assume that the antagonism between students—and sometimes teachers—is relational or interpersonal, which prevents them from exploring its social, political, and historical antecedents. There may not be opportunities to discuss antagonism between students, or teachers may want to avoid such discussions for fear they will turn into an explosive, difficult to control conversation. As we learned in our workshops, to create a climate for learning, it is critical, although difficult, for teachers or administrators to open up such conversations.

In chapter 3, about the Chester Upland School District, structural distrust was located in the hierarchical nature of power emanating from top-down and outside control of the district. In Lebanon, the contextual distrust among the principals was lateral and involved competition for scarce resources, as well as displacement.[11] This same kind of lateral distrust—distrust among students, teachers, or administrators rather than across lines established by hierarchy—often occurs when people bring historical understandings and group allegiances to new situations. Like families and neighborhoods, schools often promote fierce loyalty in order to build identity and recognition. Merging schools often entails losing symbols of identity (such as school names, football teams, or mascots) and can create uneasiness, discord, and distrust.

Unintended and unnoticed consequences of reforms, arising from bringing together groups of people with different histories and from different traditions, often prevent those reforms from taking hold. Further, the failure to acknowledge and address the distrust will make it difficult to ensure the smooth operation of classrooms and schools. Although this chapter is focused on the contextual distrust that appeared in professional development, this same form of distrust both arises from and is caused by several different kinds of reforms. While it may be difficult to recognize or address contextual distrust, its presence prevents lasting change.

5

A History of Education Reform Through the Lens of Distrust

Public schools have been increasingly under attack in the United States, as have public school teachers, teachers' unions, school boards, and district leaders, leading to the current reform movement, which seeks to replace district-run public schools with market-based alternatives such as charter schools.[1] The narrative of the persistent failure of schools and the tightening of controls on teachers has, in turn, led to a general dissatisfaction among teachers, as reflected in recent reports of low morale and discontent with the profession.[2] What does it mean for there to be growing distrust in our educational system, educational practices, and the teachers who work each day in classrooms? What are the consequences of reforms, if the changes that policy makers enact are mired in distrust, breed more distrust, or ignore the history of distrust that precedes them?

Despite current attacks on education and their attendant distrust, there remains a persistent belief in the United States that schools are critical to curing societal ills by "promoting social mobility, creating national harmony, and building solid citizens."[3] For instance, during his enactment of the Great Society initiative designed to end racial injustice and poverty, Lyndon Johnson proclaimed that: "The answer for all our national problems comes down to one single word: education."[4] Over the ensuing decades, school reformers have variously attempted to address large issues such as racism and poverty, and more education-specific goals such as curriculum, pedagogy, and the structure of school governance. The direction of school reform measures has often been in response to specific historical moments (such as the launching of the Soviet *Sputnik* satellite) and broader political movements (such as the ascendance of neoliberalism that promotes market-based reforms such as privatizing public institutions), but each moment has framed reform efforts as critical to the future of US democracy.

AN OVERVIEW OF HOW REFORM MOVEMENTS HAVE BEEN SHAPED IN THE UNITED STATES

Education reform was once considered the purview of progressives. Horace Mann is generally considered the first education reformer in the United States. As secretary of the Massachusetts Board of Education, he advocated for "universal" public schools and teacher training, claiming that schools were "the great equalizer of conditions among men." Although there were a variety of informal educational opportunities for some children during the early 1800s, especially those who were wealthy, Mann and others wanted to replace these unequal opportunities with publicly funded schools for all children.[5] Further, he advocated that children from a variety of social backgrounds should attend school together in locally developed, locally governed, and locally operated schools. As a result of this vision, there was a rapid development of public schools across the United States, meant to build a democratic society and provide equal opportunities for the citizenry; they became the foundation of today's US public school system.[6] However, it is critical to note that while the system of public schools was fundamental to the democratic vision of that time, opportunities for Native Americans, African Americans, and women were severely limited in state-sponsored schools. This remains true today, especially for many students of color.

The goal of providing equal opportunity through education, or a focus on schools as a site to produce equity, has been a central tenet of US educational policy and foundational to the practice of democracy in this country. Each successive wave of progressive educational reform has attempted to "improve" children and families, teachers and administrators, and public education itself in the name of increasing equity. In the past twenty-five years, however, the new education reformers have shifted the meaning of "reform" from a progressive vision to a neoliberal focus on "choice" and the privatization of public education as strategies for improving educational outcomes, which many people claim undermines the "public" nature of public schools.

Despite their different political and educational agendas, however, both progressive and neoliberal education reformers have generally defined, diagnosed, and sought to address the essential challenges to public education through deficit perspectives. These perspectives have in turn led to the distrust and blame, noted above, that have prevented lasting change. There are numerous examples in the last two decades alone of how new reforms or directions for educational change have begun from this stance. In his first speech on education, President Barack Obama bemoaned the fact that "despite resources that are unmatched anywhere in the world, we've let our grades slip, our schools crumble, our teacher quality fall short, and other nations outpace us."[7] Likewise, President Donald Trump proclaimed in his inaugural address that "beautiful" students are "deprived of all knowledge" by the "cash-guzzling schools" in our country.[8] His secretary of education, Betsy DeVos, has repeatedly labeled public schools as a "dead-end" bureaucracy, claiming that unionized teachers "care more about a system, one that was created in the 1800s, than they care about individual students."[9]

For the better part of the past century, politicians and commentators have complained about the state of education in the United States, while public officials, educators, and other educational advocates have promoted one reform after another, in what Amanda Lashaw has labeled the "reform industry."[10] This has been especially true since the 1960s, when the first international comparisons of achievement were published. Policy makers have variously blamed families, teachers, and the public schools themselves for the failure of the US educational system. In each case, this blame has come from a deficit perspective: critics variously contend that families don't prepare their children adequately for school or support them once they are there; that teachers care more about their jobs than the children they teach and are not capable of objectively assessing their students; or that public schools are mired in useless bureaucracies and could be more efficiently managed by the private sector, or even for-profit companies. Such views lead almost inevitably to some person or entity being held to blame for not having what is needed, which constructs that person (or persons) or entity as a target for blame, which in turn engenders distrust in both directions: toward those who are being blamed, but also from those who are being blamed toward those who blame them.

The history of educational reform illuminates the ways these circuits of blame and distrust have shaped education policy and also how policies have promulgated distrust, which has led to the current frustration, expressed by people across the political spectrum, with schools and school systems, particularly those in urban areas, which seem resistant to change. However, as I discuss throughout this chapter, two other material factors have compounded the challenge of strengthening urban public schools: the pervasiveness of poverty and the impact of structural racism, that is, the ways that racism is embedded in institutional policies and practices.

Through an analysis of key moments of educational reform in the United States over the past few decades, I argue that the failure of each reform movement to address structural inequalities is connected to its starting point. Deficit views often lead policy makers or the public at large to blame people of color or youth and families living in poverty for their failure, rather than acknowledging the structural racism and lack of opportunities they face. Without the acknowledgment of the role of poverty and racism, it becomes impossible to make sustainable change. It is both imperative—yet not sufficient—for policy makers to recognize and address distrust in formulating new policies. It is critical to simultaneously address structural racism and poverty to achieve lasting change and equitable educational opportunities for all children.

As in all social reform movements, education policy makers generally introduce new reforms in response to their dissatisfaction with the status quo. Typically, policies to reform education are narrowly focused on changing individuals (often students, teachers, and parents) and institutions (primarily public schools) rather than seeking systemic change.[11] Paralleling the three-part framework of distrust I have traced in previous chapters, this approach is another instance of how relational distrust, which is based on surface-level interactions, elides the more systemic forms of distrust—contextual and structural.

In this chapter, I examine the history of educational reform to illustrate how the three types of distrust have shaped educational policy in a way that has prevented lasting and successful change, particularly in communities that have faced the greatest challenges to educating all children. Beginning with the *Brown v. Board of Education* ruling, I illustrate the cycles of blame and distrust that have impeded reform through three of the central educational reform movements of the last seventy-five years aimed at increasing equity and access to schooling. The first two of these reform movements—strategies that focus on the achievement of equal opportunity and access to schooling for all students, as advocated by Mann, and strategies that emphasize global competitiveness through greater accountability and curricular reform—were based on a deficit view of families and teachers, particularly families and teachers of color. The failure of these reform movements led to the third movement: the current market-based reforms that threaten the future of public schools, particularly in urban communities. A focus on distrust and blame as motivations for change reveals the potential limitations of each of the reform movements and also suggests possibilities for alternative approaches, as I outline in chapter 6, where I ask what would happen if policy makers initiated education reform from an asset- or strength-based perspective or began by engaging those who have committed their professional lives to the education of our children.

GROUNDING POLICIES TO ADDRESS SOCIAL INEQUALITY IN A NARRATIVE OF BLAME

Arguing the case for paying reparations to African Americans in the United States, Ta-Nehisi Coates writes, "America begins in Black plunder and white democracy, two features that are not contradictory but complementary."[12] Describing the forced labor (slavery), devastating separation of families, and government embrace of segregation as reflected in discriminatory housing policies, Coates explains how the experiment of democracy was designed for whites through the subordination of African Americans. Tracing the journey of Clyde Ross from Mississippi to Chicago, where he lived for fifty years and still could not attain a mortgage, Coates argues that housing policies "engineered the wealth gap, which remains with us to this day."[13] He urges us to take seriously the concept of reparations that includes the acceptance of the collective history, responsibility, and consequences of the laws and practices that promoted racist policies and actions.

While Coates's analysis is built on the foundation of housing segregation and discrimination, it could just as easily have been a story about the deprivation of education and opportunity in the United States. Discrimination in housing and education policies begins with racism and the devaluing of the humanity of minoritized populations, leading to deficit views that some people are less deserving than others.[14] In the case of education, the remedies brought about by Supreme Court rulings initially focused on educating African American and white children in the same classrooms, rather than addressing the history and root causes of their unequal opportunities, namely racism and a legacy of white supremacy. While the concept of reparations in education is most often translated as affirmative action policies in education and integrated schools, Coates invites us to highlight how educational history, policies, and practices have shaped (and prevented) equal opportunity in the United States over time, which affirmative action policies will not address on their own. Although affirmative action and other measures to increase educational opportunities for African American children—and more recently for children from a range of cultural and linguistic backgrounds—were designed to address historical inequalities, their basis in deficit perspectives and distrust prevents their enduring success.

The variety of attempts (and even greater resistance) in the 1960s and 1970s to build an educational system in response to the 1954 *Brown v. Board of Education* decision and the notion that the existing system was both separate and unequal are often considered the beginning of education reform in the United States. Rather than analyzing all possible factors, such as school funding policies, these efforts framed the problem as located in the performance of African American students, which in turn shaped the proposed solutions. This deficit perspective—focused on the failure of African American children and teachers—ultimately led to the closure of African American schools and dismissal of African American teachers, which may not, in hindsight, have been the best solution for students. An analysis that included an investigation of the value of community-based and -run schools might have led to a different conclusion.[15] As illustrated below, the forced desegregation of schools instigated distrust across race lines. In addition, a consequence of desegregation policies was increased distrust of the government and officials who were charged by the Supreme Court to implement the policy.

Ten years after the *Brown* decision, the landmark 1964 Civil Rights Act mandated a large-scale social science survey to determine why African American students were not performing well in public schools. The subsequent report, *Equality of Educational Opportunity*, written by sociologist James Coleman and his colleagues, highlighted two significant findings: there was an "achievement gap" between African American and white students in the United States, and that gap was attributable to family background.[16] In particular, the report argued that the social composition of a school, as well as students' neighborhoods and their family backgrounds, determined their academic achievement. The complex set of findings from this report were reduced by the media to the idea that African American children would have a higher degree of success if they went to school with their white peers. The report was used to promote busing and a range of school desegregation efforts. As I explain in an earlier article:

> In response to the Coleman report (1966), proponents of desegregation argued that by attending White schools, Black students would learn White, middle-class ways of acting that would enable them to improve their academic achievement and their chances to attain economic success in a White society. There was also an explicit goal, held by many as fundamental to our conception of democracy, that desegregated schools would lead to integrated residential patterns and a less racially stratified society. Black and White children sitting side-by-side in schoolrooms might translate into integrated workplaces and housing developments and ultimately to a truly pluralistic society.[17]

The goal of teaching white middle-class norms to African American children implicitly devalues the strengths of African American schools, teachers, students and communities, which functioned—and in some cases, flourished—in the face of less support, fewer resources, and entrenched racism.[18] This devaluation stems from, and ultimately leads to, greater distrust in the African American community.

Policy makers constructed the post-*Brown* policies based on their contextual distrust of the African American community, rooted in a history of slavery and the ambivalence in the United States about the necessity or advisability of the education of African American children. The policies also led to practices that reinforced a hierarchy of racial groups, increasing structural distrust between African American and white children. For instance, in Wilmington, Delaware, in 1978, the court mandated a 9–3 plan where all students spent nine years in historically white schools and three years in historically African American schools. African American children were bused to white suburbs for elementary and high school, while white children were bused to the city for middle school. When I conducted research on race and desegregation in Delaware schools, I was told that this policy reflected the fact that white parents would never send their young children to the city because it was dangerous (and predominantly African American). As a result of the *Brown* decision in Delaware and across the country, African American students left schools anchored in their communities with teachers who were committed to them and their families, and invested in their futures, joining predominantly white schools where teachers often had little knowledge of their experiences, histories, or promise as individuals.[19]

The range of desegregation efforts mandated by federal rulings in the *Brown* decision and the related court cases that both preceded and followed it were enacted in local contexts. Imposed on school systems by outsiders, in this case the judiciary, they reflected a top-down approach to addressing inequality and, as such, both emerged out of and generated distrust. Court-ordered busing and other mandatory solutions engendered relational distrust between African American and white communities and a shared structural distrust of the courts—and government—that imposed these measures. The stories of Ruby Bridges, the Little Rock Nine, and the Boston busing crisis, among others, memorialized the anger of white families forced to go to school with African American children, vividly illustrating the relational distrust generated by this set of policies. At the time, the media paid little or no attention to the response of African American families to the splintering of their communities and dissolution of their community-based schools. Each of these cases illustrate distrust in the ability of the African American community to educate its youth and a solution that was undermined by both the distrust it was based on and the distrust it engendered. Underlying the visceral relational distrust among individuals was structural distrust reflecting a history of racism and political maneuvers, as well as contextual distrust arising from intergroup tensions between African American and white communities.

When forced to desegregate, school leaders often did not provide teachers with the requisite knowledge and opportunities to learn how to address racism and the challenges of teaching students from disparate backgrounds in desegregated schools. The public then blamed teachers, students, and families for the discord in classrooms and communities, making them targets of relational distrust, rather than acknowledging that the mandates to desegregate schools did not include professional learning opportunities that might have allowed the reform to succeed and did not account for the persistence of structural racism. There was well-documented resistance to desegregation efforts in districts and communities in the north as well as the south and, as a result, few schools were actually integrated for long periods of time. Instead, white families fled to suburbs or sent their children to private schools.

Over time, in some contexts, teachers and schools have learned to address the diversity of students in their classrooms, but most schools have become resegregated due to new court challenges, housing patterns, the introduction of various forms of choice, and the fact that root causes of the tensions, including relational distrust, went unaddressed. The attempt to address a series of local problems by changing the racial composition of schools rather than recognizing and including measures to address the structural issues of poverty and racism, as well as the persistent distrust, made the fixes temporary rather than permanent. What appeared to be relational distrust was grounded in structural distrust reflecting history and politics, as well as the contextual distrust arising from the convergence of disparate communities without mediation and understanding.

While district leaders and politicians made slow, but significant, progress to desegregate US schools in the years following the *Brown* decision, in much of the country today schools are more segregated than they were immediately after the passage of *Brown*, reflecting segregated housing patterns among other factors. The UCLA Civil Rights Project reports that in the past twenty-five years, there has been a dramatic increase in the segregation by race and poverty for African American and Latinx students who are concentrated in schools whose outcomes fall well below those of middle class schools with predominantly white and Asian American students.[20] The distrust among students, families, and teachers, continues to remain unaddressed and as a result, (white) students choose to go to predominantly white schools that are often better funded.

The history of the "choice" movement goes back to closure of previously all-white public schools in the aftermath of the *Brown* decision. For instance, one Virginia country closed all of the schools in the district for five years, opening segregated white private academies and leaving African American families and children to locate their own schools. Many African American students ended up attending volunteer schools or moving to live with relatives.[21] These extreme measures reflect the extent that white families exhibited structural and relational distrust of African American students and teachers.

HOW DESEGREGATION POLICIES FOSTER DISTRUST AND BLAME

When school integration faltered, policy makers turned to legislation to boost the achievement of poor and African American children. The compensatory programs that were established by the legislation were integral to President Johnson's War on Poverty, which was designed to address the "disadvantages" children living in poverty brought to school. The language of "compensation" implies deficits that need to be addressed. In their development of compensatory programs, the writers of this legislation drew on ideas of "cultural deprivation" and the "culture of poverty" that were popular at the time.[22]

These compensatory programs, meant to boost student achievement, were also based on the well-known Moynihan report that argued that Civil

Rights laws were not enough to address inequality.[23] While Moynihan's intention was to find better ways to achieve equity, the conclusions of the report were based on a deficit analysis and stereotyping of the structure of African American families and their child-rearing practices. Designing a set of programs based on perceived deficits rather than trust reinforced blame and distrust. For instance, legislators enacted Title 1 of the Elementary and Secondary Education Act of 1965 (ESEA) to distribute funds to schools with high percentages of students who qualify for free and reduced-price lunch. These programs aimed to counter the persistent effects of concentrated poverty in urban and rural areas and racism, with the goal of improving educational opportunities for all children.[24] However, one consequence was that, in order to give them additional resources, students from impoverished backgrounds were segregated from their classmates, which often led to labeling, deficit attributions, and stigmatization.

Starting with an explicit deficit perspective and an analysis that blamed families (because of their dysfunction) led to the eventual failure of the policies that were meant to lead to greater opportunities for students living in poverty. Teachers and administrators generally distrusted the students' abilities and held students in the segregated classrooms to lower standards, making it less likely that they could take college preparation courses. If schools and teachers had instead viewed them through an asset lens that recognized their cultural knowledge and experiences located in their local community in culturally responsive ways, it is likely that youth would have been more engaged, with stronger results.[25] Rather than basing desegregation policies on lifting up one group, they may have been more successful had they been based on the notion that people learn more and have greater success when they are in multiracial settings.

The desegregation policies that grew out of the *Brown* decision, along with the compensatory policies of Civil Rights reforms, were meant to address the inequality of opportunity. What is notable is that, while the reforms were ostensibly designed to improve the educational chances for all children, they were fundamentally based on blaming children and their families for their deficiencies and compensating them for what they lack, rather than building on their strengths and engaging them in determining what they need to succeed. As a result, the emphasis has been on the child or family changing their behavior to fit into the normative classroom. Blaming individual children and families leads to relational distrust, while an asset-based approach might allow for teachers to build trust across race and class lines.

While these programs may have lifted up individuals, individual success stories, while clearly important, do not add up to systemic change. The focus on individuals, along with the lack of public will to sustain the requisite funding level to move toward equal opportunities for all students, paved the way for policy makers and politicians on both sides of the aisle to embrace market-based solutions.

TEST-BASED ACCOUNTABILITY AND DISTRUST OF TEACHERS

There have been periodic moments of education panic in US history, when the country has confronted its standing in relation to its peers. Despite the fact that our education metrics (e.g., scores from international tests) are not yet sophisticated enough to make these comparisons, in nearly every instance, the US government has responded by shifting the emphasis of its education policy. One of the first instances of such a panic followed the launch of the *Sputnik* satellite by the Soviet Union in 1957, which galvanized reforms in science and mathematics as the United States raced to catch up with its competitor. The public was afraid that the US schools were inferior to those in the Soviet Union in their math and science teaching, leading Congress to appropriate significant funding in this area. However, many of the reforms were short-lived. For instance, New Math was considered too conceptual and too difficult to teach; Man: A Course of Study (MACOS), a program developed by anthropologists and funded by the NSF, was considered too controversial.[26] As a result, both curricular reforms disappeared.[27]

Despite the gains from the reforms connected to Johnson's anti-poverty programs, in 1983, in the middle of President Reagan's first term, the National Commission on Excellence and Education issued the landmark *A Nation at Risk* report, which instigated another moment of panic. By all accounts, Reagan was taken by surprise by the report, which used bold—some would say histrionic—language to claim that "the educational foundations of our society are presently being eroded by a rising tide of mediocrity that threatens our very future as a nation and a people."[28] President Reagan had made a pledge in his 1980 campaign to de-emphasize the importance of education and disband the Department of Education. At the time, his focal educational policy was to enact legislation to allow prayer in public schools and to support tax subsidies and vouchers for parents to send their children to private and religious schools using public money. However, none of Reagan's ideas for reform were mentioned in the report, which through its dramatic statements about the status of the United States in relation to its global competitors made headline news, captured the attention of the country, and continues to have an impact on how we think about education policy today.[29]

The report famously declared: "If an unfriendly foreign power had attempted to impose on America the mediocre educational performance that exists today, we might have viewed it as an act of war."[30] The writers of the report (who were mainly academics) used the rhetoric to prompt a movement to reform the US school system to bolster our economic competitiveness.[31] It was based on a deficit view of the current state of education in the United States, highlighting its mediocrity. While education was once considered a social good connected to democratic practice, an emphasis on global competition reconceptualizes it as an economic good. The teacher's role was transformed from the preparation of students to participate in a diverse democracy to the preparation of students to be "college and career ready."[32] Once again, the report promoted distrust by focusing blame on students and teachers rather than articulating a set of reforms that would build on the strengths of US schools, as well as the capacities of teachers and students. The report boldly stated that there had been a steady erosion in the achievement of students in the United States, especially in comparison with our international competitors. This emphasis on the standing of the United States in comparison with other countries—and the focus on uniform and externally imposed standards—was ultimately detrimental to innovative pedagogical practices that take an asset lens, such as classrooms where teachers taught in ways that were responsive to the cultural and linguistic diversity of the students. For instance, when educators use an asset lens, students who speak more than one language are known as *emergent bilingual speakers*, rather than *English language learners* who need to catch up with their English-dominant peers, and teachers construct curriculum based on the knowledge students bring to school. In contrast, reforms based on external controls and remediating perceived deficits reduce curriculum to test preparation.

The government printed and distributed millions of copies of *A Nation at Risk*, and hundreds of newspaper articles discussed its conclusions. While initially, the new policies focused on state graduation requirements, course loads, assessments, and standards (e.g., *Goals 2000*), ultimately, the report ushered in a new era of federal K–12 education reforms focused on accountability measures to hold teachers and schools responsible for the high academic achievement for all students, as well as a commitment to raising academic standards.[33] As a result of its focus and the way that responsibility or blame was articulated, this report and the subsequent reforms ignited distrust in US teachers. Once again, teachers were blamed for the failure of the country to successfully compete on a global scale.

Distrust was central to the 2001 No Child Left Behind Act (NCLB), the next major federal legislation concerning education that received bipartisan support. The premise behind external accountability measures, one of the primary features of NCLB, is one of distrust. The need for an external body, distant from the local context, to evaluate a student's or a school's progress suggests a lack of trust in the teacher or school to perform this critical function. The enactment of NCLB had significant consequences for US schooling. It addressed global competitiveness by setting high benchmarks for students to meet on standardized tests. It raised the ante by adding rewards and punishments—schools would receive money only if they met those benchmarks—and decreed that the federal government would withhold money or require districts to reconstitute or close schools if they did not achieve the designated goals. As the law was originally conceived and written, all students were supposed to proceed in lockstep and meet the same high standards; it did not take into account where students had started from and, importantly, did not provide the necessary funds to support all children to get to that point. While the intent of the legislation—as indicated by its name—was to promote equal opportunity, the method, a focus on externally imposed and narrow accountability measures, rather than sufficient school funding, was harsh and unforgiving.

In a speech to the NAACP in 2000 just before the passage of NCLB, President Bush used the phrase "the soft bigotry of low expectations" to describe what he saw in Little Rock schools.[34] This phrase was subsequently repeated many times to describe the poor state of teaching in US public schools. In this same speech, Bush went on to say, "Under my vision, all students must be measured. We must test to know. And low-performing schools, those schools that won't teach and won't change, will have three years to produce results, three years to meet standards, three years to make sure the very faces of our future are not mired in mediocrity. And if they're able to do so, the resources must go to the parents so that parents can make a different choice."[35]

In this speech, the president stated clearly that the problem was that schools "won't teach and won't change," claiming that the only way to get this to happen was to test children and punish the schools if the scores were low. In his final sentence, Bush set up schools and teachers as the problem, setting the stage for vouchers and other forms of privatization to emerge as the solution.

As a result of the exclusive focus on accountability, mandates, and sanctions, there was little emphasis on rethinking teaching and learning inside of schools during this time period. As Linda Darling-Hammond and George Wood report, "While other countries are making strategic investments that have transformed schooling and produced results, we have demanded results without transforming schooling."[36] A reform based on external monitoring of teachers meant that it was difficult for schools to improve and attain the kind of results the government sought in terms of global competitiveness. At the same time, the heightened focus on test scores lessened the professionalism of teachers, making teaching a rote, rather than an intellectual, activity.

The legacy of *A Nation at Risk* is that teachers' expertise was devalued and they experienced the distrust of the policy makers and also the public at large. An extreme example of the policies that came from the blame during this time period was the introduction of scripts for teachers to read while teaching in order to standardize students' educational experience. This meant that teaching was no longer an intellectual activity responsive to the particular students in classrooms. At the same time, the distrust of teachers during the time period may have undermined their support for the new standards, influencing the success of this effort.

MARKET-BASED REFORMS AND THE EROSION OF PUBLIC TRUST IN PUBLIC SCHOOLS

Reflecting on her time in the Bush administration, Susan Neuman explained that her colleagues in the Department of Education saw NCLB as a Trojan horse for the choice agenda. The strict accountability measures, with their attendant goals that were widely recognized as impossible to achieve, were meant to highlight the failure of public education and in her words, "blow it up a bit," opening the way for privatization and school choice.[37] The distrust of education created by decades of reform purportedly designed to increase equity and opportunity for all students led the United States to the current moment, which is characterized by privatization and market-based reforms.

Today's education reformers are politicians who are concerned that the current model of public education no longer works, philanthropists and venture capitalists looking for ways to invest their money in education, and other concerned citizens who have a stake in replacing public education with a system of choice that breaks "the exclusive franchise of traditional school districts holding parents captive based on zoned attendance."[38] While earlier policy makers introduced ideas based on deficit views of children, communities, and teachers, the beliefs of this new group of reformers are rooted in a deficit perspective of the public school system, including negative views of teachers' unions, critiques of bureaucracy or centralized administration, and a belief that district-run public schools are unable to provide an excellent education for all children. Advocates for privatized and market-based reforms also include parents who do not believe their children have been or will be well served by their local public schools. Some choice advocates want local choices or individual schools that provide an alternative to the local district-run public schools; others seek districtwide change, modeled after New Orleans, which in the aftermath of Hurricane Katrina transformed its entire public school system into a network of charter schools.[39] Many of the reformers believe that private solutions and competition (implicit in the notion of choice and vouchers) will improve the marketplace of schools.

Several of the major education reforms in recent years—including charter schools, educational vouchers, tuition tax credits, and education savings plans—are based on a belief in the market as a mechanism to produce better schools. On one hand, the current education reformers argue that they introduced market-based reforms as a solution to the public's waning trust of public schools. On the other hand, critics argue that these reforms were introduced by entrepreneurs to destroy public trust of public schools in order to destroy teachers' unions and garner profits from privatized schools. With the advent of the accountability movement, which emphasized external monitoring and the shaming of teachers and schools for failing to meet external standards measured by tests, school reformers began to forge new alliances with wealthy philanthropists including Bill Gates, Mark Zuckerberg, and the Walton family, as well as strategically placed superintendents such as Michelle Rhee and Paul Vallas. Tactically, charter advocates equate their goals with those of the civil rights movement. They argue, for instance, that market-based choice benefits families of color living in poverty.[40] Conversely, they argue that any opposition to the market-based reform movement is analogous to disagreement with the civil rights movement. Scott reports that in 2004, the voucher advocacy group, D.C. Parents for Choice, aired an advertisement that compared Senator Ted Kennedy's opposition to vouchers to Bull Connor's use of dogs to attack civil rights demonstrators.[41] Today, school reformers are often labeled "corporate reformers" by those who are skeptical of their motives; targets of this label include philanthropists (referred to as "venture philanthropists") who believe in market-based reforms and both publicly and privately funded alternatives to public schools. Several large foundations have poured money into market-based reforms and, in particular, to promoting charter schools—especially in urban districts—because of their fundamental distrust of district-run public schools that have failed to produce equitable outcomes for all students.[42] The analysis that led to this conclusion neglects the impact of the persistent racism and poverty that have plagued urban systems.

Politicians have taken up the mantra against public schools, bringing the distrust of public education to a new level. While relational distrust is generally thought of as distrust of individuals, it can also apply to institutions or a set of institutions, such as public schools. For example, in 2014, New York governor Andrew Cuomo vowed to "break" public education, denouncing New York teachers and their unions and promising to enact a punitive teacher evaluation plan based on student test scores, a stance that reinforces notions of relational distrust.[43] Cuomo and others make the claim that public schools are a monopoly that should be run as a business rather than as a civic institution.[44] Beginning with a deficit view of teachers, this perspective views teacher tenure and work rules protected by unions as obstacles to improving educational outcomes, and assumes that teachers are not deeply invested in the success of their schools and their students. Not only does it lead to blaming teachers, but also blames the public school structure for the failure of schools. People's distrust of schools as institutions leads to the notion of replacing them rather than understanding what is underneath the perceived weaknesses and realizing the consequences of redirecting public funds to privately managed, and sometimes for-profit, alternatives.

In the aftermath of *A Nation at Risk*, when people were scrambling to repair a school system portrayed as broken, one group of reformers promoted standards while another advocated for choice based on free market approaches. Both reflected distrust in teachers and public schools as systems, and both were top-down solutions that left teachers out of the conversation. Among the most vocal proponents of choice as a reform were John Chubb and Terry Moe, who argue:

> Choice is a self-contained reform with its own rationale and justification. It has the capacity all by itself to bring about the kind of transformation that, for years, reforms have been seeking to engineer in myriad other ways . . . The whole point of a thoroughgoing system of choice is to free schools from . . . disabling constraints by sweeping away the old institutions and replacing them with new ones. Taken seriously, choice is not a system-preserving reform. It is a revolutionary reform that introduces a new system of public education.[45]

Chubb and Moe's language reflects the depth of their distrust in the public school system to right itself.

The promotion of student and parental choice is based on the premise that individual parent choice should supersede any notion of the common good and the promotion of democratic values that have historically been a dominant rationale for the public funding and oversight of education. Simply put, the idea of parental or school choice places the needs of individual families ahead of the idea of schools as a democratizing force in the United States. It is based on the distrust of district-run public schools and public school teachers, and in turn promotes distrust of schools and teachers.

CONCLUSION: HOW DEFICIT VIEWS UNDERMINE EDUCATIONAL REFORM

A focus on blame and distrust in educational policies highlights the tension between an emphasis on the common good—as exemplified by Horace Mann's desire to educate all children as critical for a democracy—and the belief in individual choice, illustrated by current US educational reforms. Both belief systems, which are often held in opposition to one another, are fundamental to notions of democracy in the United States. The pull between them, and the deployment of blame and distrust that come from the tension, undergird many of the current educational debates in the United States.

The tension between the public and private purposes of education have played out over and over again in the history of school reform. Missing from this debate is an analysis of the role of distrust that might illuminate why education reforms have so often failed to make lasting change. In a useful analysis of the scholarship on education reforms, David Labaree has outlined three purposes of schooling that reflect debates surrounding the role of education dating back to Horace Mann: to uphold democratic citizenship and equality; to promote social efficiency to train workers; and to provide for social mobility. While the reforms following the passage of Johnson's antipoverty legislation, including the desegregation efforts and compensatory programs, responded to this first purpose, the emphasis on accountability measures and standardization was in some ways a response to the second one. In order to produce efficient and effective workers to compete in a global marketplace, schools have been subjected to external controls. Labaree argues that the third purpose, social mobility, dominates current reform movements, given their emphasis on school choice and meeting the needs of families and children rather than the larger society as a whole.[46] What characterizes all of these reforms, however, is a deficit view of children, families, teachers, and public education that undermines the thrust of each reform by creating distrust and blame. This underlying theme is strongly felt yet rarely discussed. When education policy makers and reformers blame individuals and institutions for the failure of schools, they fail to recognize the structural causes of the failure.

In recent years, the concept of "grit" or persistence toward a long-term goal has captured the public imagination, perhaps because of its connection to the attainment of the American Dream of social mobility. Yet a focus on grit places the responsibility for change on the individual and ignores the structural factors that make it more difficult for children who attend poorly resourced schools to succeed. It keeps us from envisioning larger systemic changes in schools that might lead to more equitable conditions to insure the availability of opportunities and high-quality teaching and learning contexts for all children. It turns the public's attention away from structural and contextual factors such as poverty and racism and suggests we attend to individual achievement as our priority in improving school systems. As Christine Yeh writes: "The notion of grit has certainly spurred important discussions about the nonacademic experiences and skills we want our students to have, but it has often obscured the very conditions that created educational inequities in the first place."[47]

The inattention to the role of distrust in educational change has contributed to cycles of failure that are evident in the history of educational reform. Across the different stages of reform in the United States, and in each of the local attempts described in this book, there has been a focus on local and short-term change. At the national level, there have been too few attempts to address the seemingly intransigent structural factors such as poverty, inequality, and racism that have a significant impact on academic outcomes. When policy makers make schools responsible for solving larger societal problems, they are bound to fail. This is especially true when policy makers distrust individuals and institutions and this distrust remains unexamined. Each time there has been a shift in the focus of reforms, it has been tied to a deficit view of the stakeholder. In each instance, the proposed reform has been based on distrust—and has engendered further distrust.

At the same time that the notion of public schools is challenged by the current reformers who favor a focus on private or individual achievement, we are reminded of the importance of public schools in a democracy. Over the years, Deborah Meier has written about schools where students—and their parents, teachers, and administrators—practice democracy.[48] Similarly, Benjamin Barber has argued that public schools teach us how to be members of the public: "Public schools are not merely schools for the public, but schools of publicness: institutions where we learn what it means to be a public and start down the road toward common national and civic identity."[49] If public schools are said to be the cornerstone of a democracy, our goal should be to preserve the opportunity for all students to have engaging and uplifting educations. It behooves us as a country to learn how to do this without resorting to blame and distrust.

6

Addressing Distrust by Honoring Dignity

We live in a time of growing *precarity*, a term used by cultural anthropologists and social critics to describe the living conditions that differentially expose marginalized populations to destabilization, insecurity, and violence.[1] Anna Tsing defines precarity as "life without the promise of stability."[2] Today, the world feels increasingly precarious, with more frequent conflicts and threats of war on several continents, growing numbers of hurricanes and other natural disasters, and the mounting wealth disparities across the world. Poverty and related conditions such as homelessness, racial violence, the forcible separation of children from their parents, the unaffordability of health care, food scarcity, and underemployment increase people's feelings of precarity.

In this final chapter, I give examples of strategies for addressing distrust that include: recognizing the capacities of teachers to lead their own professional development; crafting whole-district reform with communities, including teachers, rather than imposing it from the top down; and creating community schools and educational spaces that honor and support the dignity of the youth and adults who work there. All of these strategies take time. Allowing enough time for changes to take hold is the greatest shift we will need to make in our approach to educational reform, but it is also what will allow us the greatest opportunity for meaningful and lasting change.

INSTABILITY, DISTRUST, AND CURRENT CONDITIONS OF SCHOOLING IN HIGH-POVERTY COMMUNITIES

The conditions that lead to distrust in education contexts are closely tied to this notion of precarity. The precarity that infuses people's lives around the globe—at the US border; throughout informal Syrian refugee settlements in Lebanon; in Yemen, where millions of people are fleeing their homes because of increased violence—leads to insecurity and distrust. In these communities and far too many others, children are not able to attend school regularly and don't know where their next meal will come from or even when they will see their family or caretakers. Children living in these conditions bring their distrust to school, making it difficult for them to focus on learning and succeed in academic contexts. At the same time, the underlying distrust felt by many people in the United States and around the world, caused by policies that disregard the dignity of human lives, creates unstable, precarious conditions that destabilize life in communities and in schools.

Schools located in high-poverty, marginalized communities, in particular, are characterized by disruptions and unpredictability, especially as compared with the smooth-running schools in wealthier communities. In unstable, precarious communities, both teachers and students move around more frequently, and students are forced out of schools because they are failing, their families are evicted, or their schools are closed down. Recent educational reforms, including federal, state, and local policies, have only exacerbated the disruptions caused by closing schools, replacing teachers, and exchanging meaningful inquiry- or project-based work for rote memorization.[3] The closure of district-run schools and subsequent growth of charter schools, particularly those run by external management companies, have broken the ties between schools and their communities, as well as the historical relationships between schools and communities. In the United States, children from immigrant families, particularly those who are undocumented, return home each day without knowing whether they will find their families deported or incarcerated. All of this leads to increased distrust and undermines the possibility for educational change.

The key to responding to the educational distrust that arises from the uncertainty of our times is to directly address the precarious conditions that characterize far too many schools in high-poverty communities through recognizing the dignity of youth, their families and communities, and teachers. We can do this by creating educational spaces within and outside of schools that explicitly address educational distrust and build on the capacities and experiences of youth, teachers, and leaders. This will allow our young people to be better prepared to address the challenges faced by our country and our world. It will also allow educators and policy makers to enact lasting changes in schools and districts.

* * *

Too often, educational reformers suggest quick fixes—close a school, remove a disruptive child or noncompliant teacher, implement a new standardized curriculum or packaged program, increase oversight and monitoring—rather than looking for longer-term solutions. Each of these solutions is fundamentally based on a deficit view of students, teachers, and schools. To address the precarity that permeates our lives, particularly in urban areas, and to honor the dignity of those who attend and work in schools, we can begin by recognizing and building on the strengths of individuals and institutions. By recognizing the knowledge teachers bring to classrooms, building on local experience and expertise through collaboration rather than imposing top-down solutions, creating and nurturing a culture of respect for students, teachers, school administrators, and community members, and recognizing and building on the capacities youth bring to school, it is possible to replace a culture of systemic distrust built over time by creating spaces that honor human dignity.

RESTORING DIGNITY TO TEACHING: HONORING TEACHERS' KNOWLEDGE AND EXPERIENCE

As a young teacher in Philadelphia, I was fortunate to join the Philadelphia Teachers Learning Cooperative (PTLC), a group of predominantly public school teachers from schools across the city, who have met weekly at each other's houses since the 1970s. We used a set of oral inquiry processes created by Patricia Carini, founder of the Prospect Center for Education and Research, along with her colleagues, to develop deep and nuanced understandings of children, teaching, and larger educational issues.[4] My participation in this group shaped my understanding of teaching as fundamentally based on recognizing and building on children's capacities, a practice I have since used in every aspect of my professional life.

Although this group did not explicitly use the frame of trust and distrust for their work, the time and space created by our meetings, the collaborative nature of the discussions—led by a different teacher each week—together with the predictability of the structured processes that respect teachers' expertise and children's capacities, created a counterpoint to the sometimes harsh teaching conditions in the district. The focus on teachers as leaders of their own professional growth allowed group members to address the structural distrust within the district, which had been shaped by politics and a history of administrators making decisions without bringing teachers into the conversation. For instance, when the School District of Philadelphia (SDP) replaced opportunities for teaching reading using literature with mandated materials and a prescribed curriculum in the late 1990s, the group examined how their methods for teaching reading could work in this new context. At one of the meetings, a teacher described how she had taught children who had made it to the fifth and sixth grades without being able to read a word. "I'd stand next to the child—it was usually a boy—for five minutes at the end of each day and together we would chant the words of a song or book. Through the sound and rhythm and predictability of our work together, that child, and those children, would begin to make the connections and learn to read."[5]

Together, the group developed the vocabulary to explain this process in the language of the district curriculum, so that if the teachers were questioned about their teaching practices, they had a set of responses. We collectively found a way to address the structural and relational distrust of the district that mandated a curriculum, sometimes with a script that contained instructions in what teachers had to say in each lesson, rather than believing teachers had the expertise to know how to teach children. As we worked together to create new knowledge and learn from one another, we developed new strategies for teachers to bring back to their schools.

Descriptive processes are a set of inquiry practices that teachers use to develop a collective understanding of how to teach children by building on their strengths and interests. These practices, which are at the core of the work of the PTLC, take time to develop. For instance, the group will spend over two hours discussing a single child through a set of categories designed to highlight that child's stance toward learning in great detail. Carini describes the value of looking deeply and collectively at children's work to discover their capacities for learning. As she explains, this happens when an individual or group spends time on the process: "Slowness: to pause. Slowness: to linger. Slowness: to practice acts of attention. Attending, to learn to see in the child's dancing, the child's storytelling, the child's painting, the child's construction—in the child's play—how this child particularizes and selects the world, learning it actively and in the process of that making, making her own self as well."[6]

Time, collaboration, and attention, along with a respect for the expertise of teachers and students, are essential for addressing distrust. The PTLC was initiated and led by teachers for teachers, in sharp contrast to typical top-down professional development. The PTLC's nearly forty-year history attests to its importance in teachers' lives. Made possible through the development of trust over time and through collaborative work, this set of practices addresses the structural distrust of the district, where power is more frequently located with administrators and where there is often a legacy or history of distrust. Most importantly, the practices recognize and uphold the dignity of teachers and children.

Across the country, teachers have developed similar teacher-led professional development and support groups, often connected to political action, such as the Teacher Action Group (TAG) and the Caucus for Working Educators (WE), both in Philadelphia, and Unafraid Educators in Boston. Several of these groups have been formed as alternatives to the more traditional teacher unions; others are groups within the unions to provide support for both political action and classroom practices led by teachers for teachers. Some of these groups offer time and space for teachers to read together and strengthen their participation in educational policy making. Some provide alternative solutions and materials rather than directly confronting district leadership, using an asset-based approach that often counters the country's growing distrust toward teachers and teachers' unions.

In addition, these new teacher activist groups often partner with student, parent, and community organizations to participate in the transformation of individual schools or districts.[7] By working with colleagues and community allies and taking a long view of change, they are able to address the structural distrust they so often experience from administrators and district offices as teachers in large urban systems and the contextual distrust of different community groups that can prevent change from occurring.

ADDRESSING DISTRUST THROUGH COMMUNITY ENGAGEMENT IN REFORMS

The top-down policies of school districts and building administrators often exclude the community as well as teachers in constructing solutions. This approach conveys a fundamental disrespect and relational distrust for community expertise. In addition, policies of this kind generate new structural, contextual, and relational distrust. To capture the challenges as well as the opportunities for addressing systemic distrust and creating conditions for lasting educational change, I look at contrasting stories of school reform in Newark and Union City, New Jersey. These two cities, just miles apart, both have school systems that serve mostly African American, Latinx, immigrant, and low-income communities, but took very different approaches to educational reform.

Newark: A Case of Distrust Emanating from Top-Down Reform

The story of the attempt at education reform in Newark is well-known because of its failure despite enormous financial resources and the involvement of ambitious, high-profile politicians. The project attracted national attention in 2010 when Facebook founder Mark Zuckerberg appeared on television, along with Newark mayor Cory Booker and newly elected governor Chris Christie, to make a $100 million donation to reform Newark public schools. Booker had recently given Christie a confidential proposal to reform the district's schools and make Newark the charter school capital of the nation. With Zuckerberg's grant and the promise of matching dollars from major foundations and individuals, Booker and Christie, each with an eye toward national office, hoped to draw on outside expertise to create a national model of how to reform an entire school district.[8] The decision to ignore the local expertise, in particular, landed hard on the Newark community, reinforcing a sense that after abandoning the city following the race riots in 1967, white outsiders were once again going to take control of their schools.[9] This initial structural distrust led to community resistance to the approach taken by the Zuckerberg Foundation.

In 2011, Booker appointed Cami Anderson, a former Teach for America executive, as Newark superintendent. Anderson's actions deepened the community's distrust. Almost immediately, she introduced several different school reforms in a relatively short period of time, most notably her One Newark Plan, which was designed to eliminate neighborhood schools, replacing them with a citywide lottery system that provided parents with the choice of both district-run and charter schools in a single list. This was a major change for many families, as Newark was a city where most students walked to their neighborhood school. As described in chapter 4, bringing youth together in schools from disparate neighborhoods and communities led to contextual distrust. In response to complaints from the community, Anderson claimed that she couldn't work with parents because her plan was too complex for them to understand, and she eventually stopped attending board meetings because of the anger she encountered from the crowd. The relational distrust between Anderson and the community went two ways. In April of 2014, seventy-seven members of the clergy published a position statement on Anderson's One Newark plan, calling for a moratorium on its implementation because of the instability it created in the school system and the lives of children and families in the city.

By May of that year, the city council, supported by mayoral candidate and Central High School principal Ras Baraka, unanimously passed a resolution to place a moratorium on Anderson's initiatives until she produced evidence of their success. In the end, the top-down model of change—along with the infusion of external money to pay outside consultants with little or no connection to the city, the time pressure to accomplish the change quickly, and the focus on disruption rather than increasing stability and building on local knowledge—led to increased structural, contextual, and relational distrust and little academic progress in the schools.

Several aspects of this initiative, most notably its top-down imposition on the community by outsiders and its fast pace dictated by the career ambitions of politicians, created insurmountable structural distrust among the teachers, school administrators, and community members. Today, despite the massive infusion of dollars, Newark Public Schools continue to struggle. Zuckerberg has moved on to other school reform ideas and Booker is in the US Senate. The failure of this concerted effort to reform the Newark school system mirrors what happened in Oakland and cities across the United States. The strategy of imposing top-down decisions and pushing the community out of the way to reform the schools led to increased alienation, paralyzing distrust, and precarious reforms.

Union City: Educational Change That Recognizes the Expertise of Teachers and the Community

In contrast to Newark, Union City took a slower route to change, grounded in community participation and a respect for teacher knowledge. Union City is a small city that is ranked as one of the poorest and most crowded cities in the country, with an unemployment rate almost 50 percent higher than the average in the United States. It is predominately Latinx, with a large number of recent immigrants from Ecuador. Threatened by state takeover in 1989 because of its failing schools, the district dramatically turned itself around and avoided Newark's fate of state takeover in 1995 (that lasted until 2017).

New York Times journalist and Berkeley professor David Kirp was drawn to study the city's school system because of its nationally recognized preschool programs. In the district, he found a reform story that stands in clear contrast to Newark. When threatened by a state takeover, the superintendent of Union City embarked on a local strategy that engaged the community, the principals, and the teachers, addressing the kind of distrust that hampered progress in Newark. In contrast to the high speed and high-profile approach in Newark, Union City took what Kirp characterized as a slow and steady approach to reform.[10]

The architect of the Union City reform plan was Fred Carrigg, a veteran teacher who worked with his teacher colleagues to develop an approach to district reform that addressed distrust by beginning with a focus on how students learn best, how to support teachers to teach well, and how to engage parents in their children's education. For instance, the district changed its approach to teaching emergent bilingual students, initiating a program to teach students initially in their native language, building on that knowledge as an asset rather than seeing it as a deficit to be overcome, and hiring more teachers who spoke Spanish or who had ESL training. The district focused resources on the youngest children, providing programs for all three- and four-year-olds.

In addition to a strong teacher role in crafting the vision of the district, there was stable leadership at the district level and from the city's mayor, Brian Stack. Each of these decisions explicitly addressed all three kinds of distrust—contextual, structural, and relational—that had been building in the district. The district leaders addressed contextual distrust by creating opportunities for teachers and communities to work together across race, class, and linguistic differences and by taking into account the histories various groups brought to their schools. Engaging teachers as leaders in the reform process and allowing them to take on significant roles in developing the directions of the new policies, led to the dissipation of structural distrust between those with power (the district administrators and mayor) and the teachers and community members. In addition, there are no charter schools in the district—schools that often have ties to outside management organizations—and there was no move to either close down "underperforming schools" or replace local teachers with Teach for America recruits. This meant that teachers, administrators, students, and community members did not have to fight to keep their schools open, a situation that often leads to relational distrust with the district, as happened in Newark. According to traditional metrics, Union City schools are currently doing well: their test scores are the highest of all New Jersey cities, student attendance and graduation rates have increased, and students are asking to transfer into its schools.[11]

* * *

What are the lessons from Union City and Newark? David Kirp concludes that the "slow and steady" approach and the absence of pizzazz were critical components of Union City's success. The district developed a long-term set of strategies that addressed the educational needs of children beginning in preschool and continuing through high school graduation. People often point out the high enrollment in public prekindergarten as key to its success. Across the district, and across all grade levels, teachers create nurturing spaces for learning while holding their students to high expectations. As Kirp explains: "A quarter-century ago, fear of a state takeover catalyzed a transformation. The district's best educators were asked to design a curriculum based on evidence, not hunch. Learning by doing replaced learning by rote."[12]

I would add that this set of reforms was not only built on trust, but also addressed the various forms of distrust that so often accompany school reform by focusing on long-term goals, working toward stability rather than disruption as a force for change, and creating and nurturing a culture of respect for youth, teachers, school administrators, and community members. By drawing on the ideas and leadership of the community to envision change, the dignity of each person and the recognition of their expertise was upheld. There were no quick solutions and imposition of ideas from outsiders who had no plans for long-term investment in the community. Rather, there were carefully considered, respectful solutions that began to address deeper systemic challenges and persistent distrust that are often present in poor, predominantly immigrant, African American, and Latinx communities in the United States.

What might have happened in Newark if, instead of dismissing local participation, the leaders had assumed that the community had the requisite knowledge and experience to participate in the change process? Rather than imposing change from the top-down, the leaders might have implemented reforms that built on and respected local expertise through collaborative processes, while providing enough time for the local stakeholders to adapt the reforms to their particular contexts. Importantly, this approach would be more likely to address the distrust that so often stands in the way of education reform. In the following sections, I briefly describe several educational reforms that provide examples of how schools, districts, and other educational spaces can provide opportunities for teaching and learning that addresses distrust and promotes lasting education change.

FREEDOM SCHOOLS: CREATING EDUCATIONAL SPACES THAT HONOR STUDENTS' DIGNITY

Far too many African American youth currently attend schools in the United States that are underresourced and do not use culturally affirming practices that draw students into learning. And far too many youth and their families distrust the current schools their children attend. In contrast, Freedom Schools—an educational reform designed to increase literacy learning and prevent summer reading loss for African American youth—provide an example of an alternative educational space based on the idea that all students have the capacity to learn. Staffed primarily by college students and recent college graduates, Freedom Schools are located in eighty-seven cities across the country.

The inspiration for these schools comes from the Freedom Schools that were initiated by the Student Nonviolence Coordinating Committee (SNCC) during the 1964 Freedom Summer in Mississippi.[13] They were six-week programs designed to prepare disenfranchised African Americans to become active and engaged citizens by teaching them strategies of resistance and protest.[14] The African American high school students who attended them used these tactics to protest their educational conditions when they returned to their schools after the summer.[15]

With a greater focus on literacy, the current version of Freedom Schools initiated by the Children's Defense Fund (CDF), draws on many of these same practices.[16] The schools are six-week literacy enrichment summer programs whose teaching practices are based on the principles of respect, justice, and learning through the recognition of the strengths of individuals. As Tyrone Howard, professor of education and director and founder of the Black Male Institute at UCLA, explains, the schools affirm students' dignity and humanity.[17] The curriculum is based on the idea that all children should feel respected in order to learn. The five essential components of the Freedom Schools are: high-quality academic enrichment; parent and family involvement; social action and civic engagement; intergenerational servant leadership development; and nutrition, health, and mental health.

Grounded in a history of African American activism and solidarity, as well as practices that affirm cultural identity, the Freedom Schools provide opportunities to repair the various kinds of distrust that youth may have experienced in their prior years of schooling, while giving them academic confidence and strength in their identities as scholars to return to their schools with a greater sense of agency. This approach can serve as a model for how to create dignity for all students in educational spaces, whether in traditional schools or community contexts. By affirming students' dignity and teaching in culturally sustaining ways, schools and educational programs like the current Freedom Schools are able to counter the violence and contextual distrust that far too many youth encounter in school, replacing the zero tolerance policies that criminalize youth with policies and practices that address the distrust youth too often bring into formal educational spaces.

Through an asset-based approach, the teachers in these schools teach the students and provide them with experiences that build on their considerable knowledge and experience, often unrecognized in their traditional classrooms. Understanding their own power and areas they can assert control allows students to overcome structural distrust and be more open to learning. Through reading literature that affirms their identities and futures, the students and teachers can address the relational distrust that so often characterizes their experiences in school. And by teaching political organizing skills, the Freedom Schools address structural distrust that characterizes the power imbalances in schools and school systems.

COMMUNITY SCHOOLS: TRUSTING AND BUILDING ON THE CAPACITIES OF STUDENTS

Like Freedom Schools, community schools are an example of an educational reform that embraces the concept that the people who teach students should include the wider community, which has a strong investment in the education of its youth. In addition, similar to the philosophy that undergirds Freedom Schools, community schools—generally public schools that have embraced a wider mission—often address structural distrust by providing a broad array of resources for students and their families that affirm their humanity.

Community schools include services and educational programming for adults as well as children, breaking down boundaries of who is included and who is excluded from school learning. Researchers from the National Education Policy Center (NEPC) and the Learning Policy Institute (LPI) found that there are four central components of community schools: integrated student supports; extension of learning time and opportunities; family and community engagement; and collaborative leadership and practices.[18] As described in chapter 2, a strategy initiated by Superintendent Tony Smith in 2009 created several full-service public community schools in Oakland. Recently, several of these community schools, including Oakland International High School, have been called on to create educational opportunities for a newly arrived group of youth—unaccompanied minors.

Beginning in 2013, unaccompanied minors grew to be about a quarter of the students at Oakland International High School, with most arriving from Guatemala. Many of the students have interrupted schooling and many, especially the young women, have not attended school beyond the elementary grades. The youth often traveled to the United States on their own, risking dangerous border crossings or abuse by human traffickers, as well as detention and deportation by Mexican and US law enforcement officials. Although some youth leave their countries to escape poverty, in recent years, many have come to the United States to flee extreme violence and the presence of gangs and drug cartels in their home countries.

Too often, youth who have experienced traumatizing events and extreme poverty are only seen through a lens of trauma (and deficit), and thus are difficult to teach, rather than as students who have a tremendous amount to teach their classmates, bringing important strengths and knowledge to their classrooms. An understanding of how to teach this group of students and provide supportive educative contexts that allow them to learn is instructive for developing solutions to address distrust more broadly in schools and community-based educational contexts.

Two examples of how educational settings have responded to the contextual, structural, and relational distrust the unaccompanied minors bring to their educational settings—one inside a school and one in an out-of-school setting and both in Oakland—illustrate how schools and programs can implement strategies that build on youth's capacities and insights, while treating the students with dignity and respect. The set of responses developed by the teachers and staff are instructive for teachers, schools, and districts who teach new immigrant students, as well as other students who have experienced precarity in their home, community, and school lives.

The first example comes from Oakland International High School (OIHS), a community school that is part of a national network of schools (the Internationals Network for Public Schools). The entire student body of OIHS comprises recent immigrants from about thirty-five countries. The second, briefer example comes from an afterschool program designed for new immigrants that provides the youth with tools and media to tell their stories. Each example represents an educational approach that addresses distrust and is instrumental for fostering educational change.

Oakland International High School: Practices to Address Distrust as a Community School

Adults, whether teachers or leaders of community-based programs, are often at a loss as how to address the vast needs of groups of immigrant youth, especially unaccompanied minors, who bring significant distrust to their daily interactions, including contextual distrust, given the vast differences between their homes of origin and their new communities. The four characteristics of community schools described above have been central to the ability of Oakland International High School to address these various forms of distrust. As a community school, OIHS integrates several social support systems into its academic life, including social workers, counselors, mentors and tutors, afterschool programs, and access to legal and healthcare services. However, these additional services are often not enough for the youth, who may not feel welcome in their new homes, have huge debts to pay off, face pending court cases that could result in their deportation, and are often scared. As Carmelita Reyes, an OIHS founder and coprincipal, explained, "They have used up all of their resiliency."[19]

OIHS uses its community focus in order to address distrust, implement an asset-based approach, and forge deeper relationships with their students by better understanding the knowledge and experience they bring to their education. Several years ago, the school instituted a professional development practice called "community walks" in which students introduce the teachers and staff to the their home communities and cultural knowledge. The walks all follow a particular sequence and include lunch at a restaurant that serves food from the students' home country. One district professional development day in the fall is set aside for this activity and every faculty and staff member, including the janitorial staff and librarian, participates. The school leaders invite about seven students from various ethnic and cultural backgrounds to lead the walks, and each adult in the school is assigned to one of the seven walks.

For example, one of the community walks several years ago was led by Angel, who had recently arrived from Guatemala as an unaccompanied minor. Angel began his walk by giving the participants an excerpt from a book about the journey of an unaccompanied minor, who had a story that was dramatic and similar to his own.[20] He also showed several film clips that depicted issues faced by immigrant students in their home countries, such as teen pregnancy. Next, there was a panel, moderated by one of the counselors who is fluent in Spanish, that included three boys who narrated the stories of their harrowing journeys. (No one forces students to tell their stories, and most choose not to do so in public forums.) The group then embarked on their community walk, stopping first at a legal clinic that provides counsel to the students about their court cases and then to a shelter run by Catholic Workers that several of the youth in the school had stayed in when they first arrived. Finally, they were joined by other students and families for lunch at a local Guatemalan restaurant.

When Angel first entered the school, his teachers described him as constantly angry. They never knew if he would respond to a simple question with a long string of expletives and walk out of their classrooms or if he would respond politely. He did not seem to trust anyone. His stance toward school changed, however, after he led his community walk. The process of connecting his teachers and the school staff to his new community and to his home cultures, seemed to dissipate some of his contextual distrust. He became calmer and more consistently engaged in the larger community.

The school addresses the contextual distrust that youth bring with them to school in a systemic way that starts with the assumption that the youth have knowledge that is worthy of sharing with the adults in the school. Teachers pay close attention to the students in their classrooms and attempt to create bridges between their knowledge and what they need to know to learn the academic subjects. The community walks affirm their knowledge and experiences and provide opportunities for leadership. The school offers various social support services for the youth, the community liaison who accompanies them to their court cases, and many different people to listen to their fears. It gives the youth time to adjust and enter the new community, pairing them with students who have been in school longer and may have developed useful strategies.

As the school works to develop relational trust with the students, the staff also realizes that the contextual distrust they bring to school is systemic. That means that while students may not directly talk about the history of violence and terror they have experienced, these realities are part of their current lives that teachers and administrators must take into account as they create opportunities for them to learn and succeed in school. At times, the only way for the teachers and counselors to address the distrust might be to simply listen without immediately offering solutions. In addition, it is important to learn about the strengths, knowledge, and experience students bring to classroom learning in order to find asset-based ways to teach them. It is also critical to give these students the time they need to develop relationships and trust.

Lauren Markham, the Community School Program Manager, who spent years as a journalist in El Salvador and on the border, explained that by the time the students arrive at school, they have experienced a series of powerless situations.[21] When they feel powerless, especially as adolescents, they act out and attempt to regain a modicum of power and control over their lives in response to their structural distrust, as Angel did. In addition, they often enter the school in the middle of the semester and are confused and lost. They distrust authority figures. When a teacher tells students that they can't have a cell phone, they often feel as though it's a police officer giving that command and they respond fiercely. Even when teachers or administrators have developed strong relationships with the youth, they can quickly flip to anger, distrust, and resentment, which can feel surprising because the teachers have spent so much time building relationships.

The community school framework provides additional resources for teachers to address the distrust students bring to school, but the hard work often takes place in the classrooms. Addressing relational distrust through building strong relationships and interpersonal or collective trust is often not enough. One possibility is for teachers to work with the students to understand the history of the contextual distrust they bring with them without forcing them to recount their stories either in writing or in conversation. Possible strategies include hearing or reading other stories told by or about youth in similar situations, studying the events that led to the political and social conditions that forced them to leave their countries, and seeing their own role as actors in this history.

Another approach is to study how power operates in their school, home, and community in order for them to understand where they may be able to have agency or control in their lives. Understanding where youth realistically have control can allow them to feel more secure or in charge of their lives. At OIHS, progress is always slow and though many students drop out, the school always works hard to keep the students as long as it can. Because OIHS is a community school, students often drop back in or teachers find them on the streets and convince them to return for at least a few months. The entire school works together to support their learning and future opportunities for the time they are in school, knowing that the period of time may not last long. Still, teachers and staff are patient and work with an eye to the future, while being immersed in the present. Although other schools and districts may not work with this particular population of young people, the strategy of seeing youth through their strengths and creating curriculum and activities that actively honor and use their assets is critical to addressing the various kinds of distrust that so many youth bring to school.

Urgent Art: Expressing Knowledge and Experiences in an Afterschool Program

Artist Caleb Duarte, who has worked with youth and adults in a wide range of settings, recently led an afterschool program in Oakland called Urgent Art. This program is an example of how youth leaders have worked successfully with unaccompanied minors in out-of-school educational spaces, and illustrates new possibilities for how to address distrust in varied contexts. The Urgent Art project involved ten new immigrant students from

Guatemala who attend Fremont High School and who primarily speak Mam, their indigenous language. Duarte explained that he uses the visual arts to create a space for expression where language may not be adequate. In his work with youth, trust often grows in the spaces between words. Duarte's projects take place in an out-of-school context, which he feels helps break down the institutional barriers and gives him the opportunity to work in a more fluid manner with the youth. In this particular program, he introduced youth to essay writing, painting, sculpture, and mask making. Together, they created magical realism performances and installations that represent their cultures and communities, beginning to dismantle some of the contextual distrust they have carried across borders and into their homes and schools in the United States. Their artwork is simultaneously a public and private statement. One afternoon, the group constructed a thirty-foot red ladder that they brought to a local art festival. Duarte explained that the ladder symbolized their quest for success, their memories of climbing over a wall at the border, their fears of death from falling, their image of escaping from prison, and more.[22]

Using this program as a model, educators can reimagine sites that build on community knowledge and engage community members as collaborators and colleagues in the education of their children. These kinds of activities also suggest ways to acknowledge and build on history through a range of media and modalities. Rather than simply building trust or community, as an artist, Caleb Duarte directly addresses the various kinds of distrust youth bring to their learning by giving them opportunities for expression that reach beyond words. Further, he uses their knowledge to create products that gives them pride.

The youth working with Duarte make powerful statements in a range of media to represent their experiences, beginning to address the contextual distrust they have experienced when they hid in their home countries, afraid to go to school because of threats made by gangs, or their precarious journeys to the United States. They also represent their daily experiences in classrooms and schools. The education of this group of youth, and many like them who have experienced various kinds of trauma, begins—through multiple modalities, words and silence, text and artistic representations—to dispel the contextual, structural, and relational distrust in their lives. The art they create reflects their capacities for learning and making statements that schools can build on in their curriculum.

RESPONSES TO PRECARITY AND DISTRUST

Each of the examples in this chapter illustrates ways to address the distrust that impedes educational change: recognizing the capacities of teachers to lead their own professional development; engaging the community in crafting reform strategies in contrast to top-down approaches; creating schools and educational spaces that preserve the dignity of the youth and adults who work there; and building change based on the capacities, experiences, and knowledge youth bring to school.

It is essential to recognize that each of these strategies takes time. As a society, we are often impatient for change, and this often leads to distrust. In several chapters, I have described how education as change has failed because it either proceeded too quickly (as was the case in Newark) or it wasn't given enough time to take hold (as happened in Oakland with the small schools and the community schools movements). It takes time to engage multiple stakeholders in new processes and to build respectful processes that honor multiple perspectives.

Throughout the book, I have described several ways that contextual, structural, and relational distrust are intertwined and too often preclude sustained educational change. In addition to the distrust present in our education systems, there is increasing distrust of various kinds in the United States. For instance, there is growing distrust of the media manifest in claims of fake news that cause people to distrust what they read or hear in the news. Undocumented children go to school each day filled with fear and distrust that their parents might be taken away at any moment by Immigration and Customs Enforcement. At the border between Mexico and the United States, US officials have begun to forcibly take children away from their parents, creating distrust at an early age. Recently, there have been frequent complaints about internet security breaches and invasions that cause people to question whether their data are protected. Various sectors distrust the government and seek local solutions, while others distrust local control because of the racial or ethnic biases which might be unchecked without government oversight. Public narratives of sexual misconduct have led women to distrust men and Catholics to distrust the church. All of this distrust adds to the precarity that shapes so many people's lives at this time in history, at the same time that the uncertainty or precarity creates conditions for distrust.

The solutions that I have proposed in this chapter for addressing distrust in educational systems—to honor the knowledge of teachers and capacity for learning of children, to build solutions with the community defined broadly rather than imposing solutions on people, and to create spaces that promote people's dignity—could be applied to the pervasive distrust in the United States and much of the world. These persistent challenges are unlikely to be addressed through building trust so that people "get along" or through quick activities and building trust on at a surface level. All depend on understanding and addressing power differentials and policies that emphasize the imbalance. Each issue also reinforces the idea that it is critical to begin by naming the distrust and then working through various systems to address the harm. The #MeToo movement began with a similar idea of naming individual perpetrators and telling stories to the public. This is not to say that these ideas and movements are comparable, but rather to suggest that it is beneficial to look across them to find new ways into addressing challenges in education.

CONCLUSION: WORKING TOWARD POSSIBILITY AND CHANGE

> [What is meant by teaching as possibility in dark and constraining times] is a matter of awakening and empowering today's young people to name, to reflect, to imagine, and to act with more and more concrete responsibility in an increasingly multifarious world. At once, it is a matter of enabling them to remain in touch with dread and desire, with the smell of lilacs and the taste of a peach. The light may be uncertain and flickering; but teachers in their lives and works have the remarkable capacity to make it shine in all sorts of corners and, perhaps, to move newcomers to join with others and transform.[23]
>
> *Maxine Greene*

These are indeed "dark and constraining times" where distrust often seems to be more prevalent than trust. Though Maxine Greene wrote this statement in the late 1990s, she could have written it today, just over twenty years later. Like Greene, I believe that teaching is a complex, and sometimes daunting, task that requires that we acknowledge the darkness, while staying in touch with the moments of sweetness, light, and possibility. As I have stated throughout this book, our current education policies too often arise from or create distrust, prompting the darkness to descend on teaching. Distrust impedes learning and change. When people work to address distrust at any level (at the policy level or in school buildings as district superintendents, as school board members, professional development leaders, administrators, teachers, community members, or students), they too often simply work to build, or rebuild, relational trust. I argue that this move, while desirable, is not enough.

Too often the solution is to bring people together to talk together or engage in activities like trust circles. Such activities build community and good will, but they may not address the underlying causes of the distrust, which are often rooted in history and politics. Understanding and naming politics and power is connected to both contextual and structural distrust. Addressing structural distrust—which emanates from top-down and outside control—begins with acknowledging and supporting local control, whether it is local governance, such as a local school board, community engagement in school or district decisions, or bringing in teachers as participants in or designers of their evaluations. There may be instances where top-down decisions are necessary or even desirable, such as decisions to preserve public schools over individual parent's preferences for charters. It is important, however, to understand how these decisions reinforce distrust and whether the decisions need to be unilateral rather than collaborative.

Often, the collateral damage from structural distrust is invisibility. When decisions are made in a top-down manner, some people will feel left out, unheard, and unrecognized, their voices lost in the cacophony of expert advice. The lack of recognition almost always leads to distrust. As the narrator in Ralph Ellison's novel, *The Invisible Man*, asks: "To whom can I be responsible, and why should I be when you refuse to see me? . . . Responsibility rests upon recognition, and recognition is a form of agreement."[24]

What might have happened in Newark, if Mark Zuckerberg had invested even a part of his money in processes to develop generative educational ideas that engaged local educators and community members? What would have happened if our board in Chester had invited local community members to sit with us as equal partners when we negotiated budgetary and curricular decisions? In each of these cases, would the local community members have experienced recognition and trust, leading to a different stake in the decision-making processes as well as the outcomes?

In addition, it is critical to acknowledge the knowledge and experience that both teachers and students bring to educational contexts in order to address distrust that may be deep-seated. We distrust teachers when we provide them with scripts to read instead of honoring their ability to listen to their students and understand the content and pedagogy they need to teach them. We also distrust teachers when we design professional development sessions for them that do not build on their knowledge. In addition, we too often forget children's desire to learn. By noticing the humanness of every child, we can recognize what Carini refers to as children's "widely distributed capacity" to be creators, builders, and actors in their education and their lives.[25] This attention to teachers and children and their capacities allows us to address the various kinds of distrust and recognize the democratizing potential of public education.

While the work of stabilizing the precarious living, working, and educational conditions experienced by youth, their families, and communities is critical, it is a long-term and slow process that extends well beyond the work of educators and education policy makers. In immediate terms, those seeking educational change can engage local communities in processes and practices to determine the fate of their own schools. It is essential for proponents of educational change to understand how and when their new proposals contribute to distrust, while at the same time realizing that distrust is often already present in schools and educational settings and will prevent the proposals from moving forward. As the narratives in this book suggest, leaders of change efforts often prefer to ignore or bypass an examination of history and the local context of distrust. The failure rates of reform, especially in US urban contexts, suggests that this is not a wise choice.

Perhaps most importantly, it is important to honor the dignity of youth, teachers, and leaders to address the distrust that can impede lasting educational change. The Freedom Schools emphasize this practice, as do the adults working with unaccompanied minors in Oakland. One way to begin is to make room and time for stories, especially those that reflect the history of oppression, rather than suppressing or ignoring them. In each of the larger narratives in this book—Chester, Oakland, and even Lebanon—the rush to solve problems may have circumvented the process of delving into history and allowing people to contribute their perspectives and understandings to the processes. Listening to stories, especially those that represent multiple perspectives, is critical to addressing all forms of distrust, especially contextual and relational distrust.

Nigerian writer Chimamanda Ngozi Adichie gave a highly acclaimed TED talk about the danger of a single story. Each of us, she explained, has many stories that comprise who we are and it is impossible to know or engage with a person or place without knowing those stories. She concluded, "Stories can break the dignity of a people, but stories can also repair that broken dignity."[26] There are power dynamics shaping whose stories are told and heard. All of these experiences contribute to the feelings of precarity and distrust around the world. And each contribute to a loss of dignity, hope, and possibility. It is imperative that we create schools and educational spaces that hold onto and promote each person's dignity. We can do that by knowing their stories, providing opportunities to learn multiple stories and multiple perspectives, and through this knowledge addressing the relational, structural, and contextual distrust that prevents educational change.

Notes

Chapter 1

1. Eve L. Ewing, "We Shall Not Be Moved: A Hunger Strike, Education, and Housing in Chicago," *New Yorker*, September 21, 2015, http://www.newyorker.com/news/news-desk/we-shall-not-be-moved-a-hunger-strike-education-and-housing-in-chicago.
2. Lyndsey Layton, "Are School Closings the 'New Jim Crow'? Activists File Civil Rights Complaints," *Washington Post*, May 13, 2014, https://www.washingtonpost.com/local/education/2014/05/13/1a0d3ae8-dab9-11e3-b745-87d39690c5c0_story.html.
3. Others have categorized trust in similar ways, including: Anthony Bryk and Barbara Schneider, *Trust in Schools: A Core Resource for Improvement* (New York: Russell Sage Foundation, 2002); Martin Gargiulo and Gokhan Ertug, "The Dark Side of Trust," in *Handbook of Trust Research*, ed. Reinhard Bachmann and Akbar Zaheer (Northampton, MA: Edward Elgar Publishing, 2006), 165–186; Nissim Mizrachi, Israel Drori, and Renee R. Anspach, "Repertoires of Trust: The Practice of Trust in a Multinational Organization Amid Political Conflict," *American Sociological Review* 72, no. 1 (2007): 143–165; and Sim B. Sitkin and Nancy L. Roth, "Explaining the Limited Effectiveness of Legalistic 'Remedies' for Trust/Distrust," *Organization Science* 4, no. 3 (1993): 367–392.
4. Eve L. Ewing, "Phantoms Playing Double-Dutch: Why the Fight for Dyett Is Bigger Than One Chicago School Closing," *Seven Scribes*, August 26, 2015, http://sevenscribes.com/phantoms-playing-double-dutch-why-the-fight-for-dyett-is-bigger-than-one-chicago-school-closing/.
5. Paul Caine and Sean Keenehan, "Dyett High School Hunger Strike Continues, Despite CPS Announcement," *Chicago Tonight*, September 16, 2015, http://chicagotonight.wttw.com/2015/09/16/dyett-high-school-hunger-strike-continues-despite-cps-announcement.
6. Pauline Lipman et al., *Should Chicago Have an Elected Representative School Board? A New Review of the Evidence* (Chicago: University of Illinois at Chicago, Collaborative for Equity & Justice in Education, 2015): 2–3.

7. Harry C. Boyte, "What Is Democratic Education—and Education for Democracy?" *Bridging Differences* (*Education Week* blog), October 1, 2015, http://blogs.edweek.org/edweek/Bridging-Differences/2015/10/what_is_democratic_education_-.html.
8. The Joyce Foundation, *Community Responses to School Reform in Chicago: Opportunities for Local Stakeholder Engagement* (New York: Public Agenda, 2012), http://www.publicagenda.org/files/CommunityResponsesToSchoolReformInChicago.pdf.
9. "From Riots to Renaissance: Bronzeville: The Black Metropolis," WTTW Chicago Public Radio, http://www.wttw.com/main.taf?p=76,4,4,8.
10. Emily Richmond, "Did High-Stakes Testing Cause the Atlanta Schools Cheating Scandal?" *The Atlantic*, April 3, 2013, https://www.theatlantic.com/national/archive/2013/04/did-high-stakes-testing-cause-the-atlanta-schools-cheating-scandal/274619/; Maura Pennington, "With High-Stakes Testing, Philly Cheating Scandal Is Just One of Many," (Washington, DC: Center for Education Reform, May 2014), https://www.edreform.com/2014/05/with-high-stakes-testing-philly-cheating-scandal-is-just-one-of-many/.
11. Bryk and Schneider, *Trust in Schools*.
12. For exceptions, see: Megan Tschannen-Moran and Wayne K. Hoy, "A Multidisciplinary Analysis of the Nature, Meaning, and Measurement of Trust," *Review of Educational Research* 70, no. 4 (2000): 547–593; Kurt T. Dirks, "Three Fundamental Questions Regarding Trust in Leaders," in *Handbook of Trust Research*, ed. Reinhard Bachmann and Akbar Zaheer (Northampton, MA: Edward Elgar Publishing, 2006), 15–28; Robert D. Putnam, *Bowling Alone* (New York: Simon & Schuster, 2000); David Carless, "Trust, Distrust and Their Impact on Assessment Reform," *Assessment & Evaluation in Higher Education* 34, no. 1 (2009): 79–89, doi: 10.1080/02602930801895786.
13. Tom W. Smith, Michael Hout, and Peter V. Marsden, *General Social Survey, 1972–2012* (Ann Arbor, MI: Inter-university Consortium for Political and Social Research, 2013), https://doi.org/10.3886/ICPSR34802.v1.

Chapter 2

1. Justice for Oakland Students Coalition, "Justice for Oakland Students: Hire Local, Long-term Superintendent" (online petition), https://iam.colorofchange.org/petitions/justice-for-oakland-students-demand-the-ousd-school-board-choose-a-locally-growns-superintendent.
2. Interviews with veteran district employees from November 10, 2015–August 15, 2017. All interviews were conducted in confidentiality, and the names of interviewees are withheld by mutual consent.
3. Interviews with veteran district employees from November 10, 2015–August 15, 2017; Valerie Strauss, "New D.C. Schools Chancellor Under Scrutiny for Overspending in California District He Led," *Washington Post*, November 21, 2017, https://www.washingtonpost.com/news/answer-sheet/wp/2017/11/21/new-d-c-schools-chancellor-under-scrutiny-for-overspending-in-california-district-he-led/?utm_term=.688e8427082f.

4. Gallup, "Confidence in Institutions," http://news.gallup.com/poll/1597/confidence-institutions.aspx.
5. Esteban Ortiz-Ospina and Max Roser, "Trust," *Our World in Data*, https://ourworldindata.org/trust.
6. *Oakland: The City of Opportunity*, (Oakland, CA: Oakland Chamber of Commerce, 1909), 16.
7. K. Gwynne Coburn and Pamela A. Riley, *Failing Grade: Crisis and Reform in the Oakland Unified School District* (San Francisco: Pacific Research Institute, July 2000), http://www.csun.edu/~th73110/oaklandschools.pdf. In 1987, Oakland became the center of a national debate when the school board passed a resolution stating that its schools should treat African American Vernacular (or Ebonics) as a second language, claiming that it was "genetically based." After nearly a month of controversy, the board amended its position with a statement that recognized the history, linguistic legitimacy, and richness of Black English, eliminating the call to teach it as a language. Across the country, people ridiculed the Oakland school board for this proposal.
8. Catherine Gewertz, "Jerry Brown's Next Project: Oakland Schools," *Education Week*, February 23, 2000, https://www.edweek.org/ew/articles/2000/02/23/24oakland.h19.html.
9. Robert Anderson, *The Labyrinth of Cultural Complexity: Fremont High Teachers, the Small School Policy, and Oakland Inner-City Realities* (Lincoln, NE: iUniverse, 2008).
10. For an important discussion of how a group of Latinx immigrant mothers worked with teachers and other parents to create a small neighborhood school, see Andrea Dyrness, *Mothers United: An Immigrant Struggle for Socially Just Education* (Minneapolis, MN: University of Minnesota Press, 2011).
11. Caroline Hendrie, "Small-Schools Backers Wary of Oakland Shifts," *Education Week*, June 4, 2003, http://www.edweek.org/ew/articles/2003/06/04/39oakland.h22.html.
12. Interview with OUSD employee, August 11, 2017.
13. Dean E. Murphy, "Dream Ends for Oakland School Chief as State Takes Over," *New York Times*, June 8, 2003, http://www.nytimes.com/2003/06/08/us/dream-ends-for-oakland-school-chief-as-state-takes-over.html.
14. Robert Gammon, "The Plot to Oust Randy Ward," *East Bay Express*, August 16, 2006, https://www.eastbayexpress.com/oakland/the-plot-to-oust-randy-ward/Content?oid=1081662.
15. Alain Jehlen, "Boot Camp for Education CEOs: The Broad Foundation Superintendents Academy," *Rethinking Schools* 27, no. 1 (2012), https://www.rethinkingschools.org/articles/boot-camp-for-education-ceos-the-broad-foundation-superintendents-academy.
16. Ibid.
17. Interviews with veteran district employees, November 10, 2015–August 15, 2017.
18. Katy Murphy, "Oakland School District: Is It Better Off After the State Takeover?" *East Bay Times*, July 4, 2009, http://www.eastbaytimes.com/2009/07/04/oakland-school-district-is-it-better-off-after-the-state-takeover/.

19. "Creating a Full-Service Community School District: Interview with Tony Smith, Superintendent of Oakland Unified School District" (Washington, DC: Coalition for Community Schools, October 2010), http://www.communityschools.org/assets/1/AssetManager/Tony%20Smith%20Interview%20Template2.pdf.
20. Katy Murphy, "Oakland School Closures: Is a $2 Million Savings Worth the Cost?" *Mercury News*, October 22, 2011, http://www.mercurynews.com/2011/10/22/oakland-school-closures-is-a-2-million-savings-worth-the-cost/.
21. Proposition 13 was enacted in 1978 as a statewide limit on the property tax rate at 1 percent of assessed value. This caused an immediate decrease in the amount of money available to districts through local taxes. Because districts were unable to raise taxes to pay for their schools, funding for schools decreased immediately by one-third.
22. Interview, February 18, 2018.
23. Oakland Unified School District, "Quality Schools/Intensive Support Overview," February 9, 2015, https://www.ousd.org/cms/lib07/CA01001176/Centricity/Domain/3448/OUSD%20Overview%20of%20Quality-Intensive%20School%20Programs%20UPDATED%2002.09.15.pdf.
24. In 2018, just over a year into his term as chancellor of the DC Public Schools, Wilson resigned from his position because of the distrust he engendered by breaking rules he had helped to establish for admission into the top public schools; see Perry Stein, Peter Jamison, and Fenit Nirappil, "D.C. Public Schools Leader to Resign After Skirting School Assignment Rules," *Washington Post*, February 20, 2018, https://www.washingtonpost.com/local/dc-politics/dc-public-schools-leader-to-resign-after-skirting-school-assignment-rules/2018/02/20/9b372230-1662-11e8-92c9-376b4fe57ff7_story.html?utm_term=.f4ab89a80b4e).
25. Valerie Strauss, "New D.C. Schools Chancellor Under Scrutiny for Overspending in California District He Led," *Washington Post*, November 21, 2017, https://www.washingtonpost.com/news/answer-sheet/wp/2017/11/21/new-d-c-schools-chancellor-under-scrutiny-for-overspending-in-california-district-he-led/?utm_term=.9e96936c0b13.
26. Interview, February 18, 2018.
27. Katherine Schultz, "The Problem with School Superintendents," *Washington Post*, April 15, 2013, https://www.washingtonpost.com/news/answer-sheet/wp/2013/04/15/the-problem-with-school-superintendents/?noredirect=on&utm_term=.085b330c2872
28. Edward McMilin, *Closing a School Building: A Systematic Approach* (Washington, DC: National Clearinghouse for Educational Facilities, September 2010), http://www.ncef.org/pubs/closing.pdf; Valerie Strauss, "How Closing Schools Hurts Neighborhoods," *Washington Post*, March 6, 2013, https://www.washingtonpost.com/news/answer-sheet/wp/2013/03/06/how-closing-schools-hurts-neighborhoods/?utm_term=.ca4d-28b9e9ea; Rachel Weber, Stephanie Farmer, and Mary Donoghue, *Why These Schools? Explaining School Closures in Chicago, 2000–2013* (Chicago: Great Cities Institute, 2016), https://greatcities.uic.edu/wp-content/uploads/2017/01/School-Closure.pdf.
29. Interview, August 11, 2017.

30. "Office of African American Male Achievement," Oakland Unified School District, https://www.ousd.org/Page/12225.

Chapter 3

1. This chapter is greatly informed by research conducted in Chester with Katie McGinn Luet, who was a research assistant during my tenure on the board.
2. "Quick Facts: Chester City, Pennsylvania," United States Census Bureau, http://www.census.gov/quickfacts/table/PST045215/4213208.
3. In 2018, Baughn returned as superintendent for the Chester Upland School District.
4. Francesca López, "Review of a Meta-Analysis of the Literature on the Effect of Charter Schools on Student Achievement (Washington, DC: National Education Policy Center, 2014), http://nepc.colorado.edu/files/nepc-ttr-chartermeta.pdf.
5. John Morrison McLarnon, *Ruling Suburbia: John J. McClure and the Republican Machine in Delaware County, Pennsylvania* (Newark: University of Delaware Press, 2003). In this book, McLarnon describes how from 1920 to 1975, Delaware County was run by a Republican political organization called the "war board," a secretive committee that carried out the orders of John McClure, who controlled all of the county and municipal jobs. The patronage system continued long after McClure's death in 1965.

Chapter 4

1. When we were in Lebanon, the population was estimated to be approximately four million, about 350,000 of whom were Palestinians. In the intervening years, particularly due to the influx of refugees from the neighboring Syria, the population is estimated to have grown to over six million. The number of Palestinians residing in Lebanon is contested because many are undocumented or not registered officially with the camps or the government.
2. Katherine Schultz, *Listening: A Framework for Teaching Across Differences* (New York: Teachers College Press, 2003).
3. Excerpt from "Words Under the Words" from *Words Under the Words: Selected Poems* by Naomi Shihab Nye, copyright © 1995. Reprinted with the permission of Far Corner Books; Garrett Hongo, "What For," *Yellow Light* (Middletown, CT: Wesleyan University Press, 1982); Linda Christensen, who developed the activity, uses the Hongo poem in her work with high school students in the United States (Linda Christensen, *Teaching for Joy and Justice: Re-imagining the Language Arts Classroom* [Milwaukee, WI: Rethinking Schools, 2009]).
4. Nada Al-Nashif and Samir el-Khoury, *Palestinian Employment in Lebanon, Facts and Challenges: Labour Force Survey Among Palestinian Refugees Living in Camps and Gatherings in Lebanon* (Geneva: International Labour Organization & Committee for the Employment of Palestinian Refugees, 2012), http://www.ceplb.org/public/uploads/images/Report%20-%20English(2).pdf.
5. When Lebanon won independence from France in 1943, the National Pact established that the president would be a Maronite Christian, the prime minister a Sunni Muslim,

and the speaker of Parliament a Shia Muslim. In addition, representation in parliament would reflect a ratio of 6:5 in favor of the Christians.

6. Al-Nashif and el-Khoury, "Palestinian Employment in Lebanon."
7. Sari Hanafi, "Palestinian Refugee Camps in Lebanon: Laboratories of State-in-the-Making, Discipline and Islamist Radicalism," in *Thinking Palestine*, ed. Ronit Lentin (London: Zed Books; Taylor Long, 2008), 82–100; Sari Hanafi, "Human (In)security: Palestinian Perceptions of Security In and Around the Refugee Camps in Lebanon," *Conflict, Security & Development* 10, no. 5 (2010): 673–692, doi: 10.1080/14678802.2010.511510.
8. Sari Hanafi, "Palestinians in Lebanon: Status, Governance and Security" *Accord* 24 (2012): 67–69, http://www.c-r.org/downloads/Accord24_PalestiniansinLebanon_0.pdf.
9. This is adapted from the Descriptive Review Process developed by Patricia Carini and her colleagues at the Prospect Archive and Center for Education and Research and a process I use in my work in university settings for presenting and discussing dilemmas of teaching and research practice; Patricia F. Carini, *Starting Strong: A Different Look at Children, Schools and Standards* (New York: Teachers College Press, 2001); Margaret Himley, with Patricia Carini, ed., *From Another Angle: Children's Strengths and School Standards* (New York: Teachers College Press, 2000).
10. Frederick Erickson, "Scaling Down: A Modest Proposal for Practice-Based Policy Research in Teaching," *Education Policy Analysis Archives* 22, no. 9 (2014): 3, http://dx.doi.org/10.14507/epaa.v22n9.2014.
11. Thank you to Caroline Chauncey for making this important point.

Chapter 5

1. Melia Repko-Erwin did critical initial research for this chapter. Our discussions greatly informed the analysis and direction of the chapter.
2. Emily Richmond, "Teacher Job Satisfaction Hits 25-Year Low," *The Atlantic*, February 21, 2013, https://www.theatlantic.com/national/archive/2013/02/teacher-job-satisfaction-hits-25-year-low/273383/, https://www.edweek.org/tm/articles/2012/03/07/metlife11.html.
3. Larry Cuban, "Reforming Again, Again, and Again," *Educational Researcher* 19, no. 1, (1990): 9.
4. Ibid.
5. Ira Katznelson and Margaret Weir, *Schooling for All: Class, Race, and the Decline of the Democratic Ideal* (Berkeley: University of California Press, 1985).
6. Ibid.; David B. Tyack and Elisabeth Hansot, *Managers of Virtue: Public School Leadership in America, 1820–1980* (New York: Basic Books, 1982).
7. Howard Blume and Seema Mehta, "Public Education in U.S. Falls Short, Obama Says," *Los Angeles Times*, March 11, 2009, http://articles.latimes.com/2009/mar/11/local/me-obama-education11.
8. Erika Christakis, "Americans Have Given Up on Public Schools. That's a Mistake,"

The Atlantic, October 2017, https://www.theatlantic.com/magazine/archive/2017/10/the-war-on-public-schools/537903/.

9. Ibid.
10. Amanda Lashaw, personal communication, March 2018.
11. David B. Tyack and Larry Cuban, *Tinkering Toward Utopia: A Century of Public School Reform* (Cambridge, MA: Harvard University Press, 1995).
12. Ta-Nehisi Coates, "The Case for Reparations," *The Atlantic*, June 2014, https://www.theatlantic.com/magazine/archive/2014/06/the-case-for-reparations/361631/.
13. Ibid.
14. Michael Katz, *The Undeserving Poor: From the War on Poverty to the War on Welfare* (New York: Pantheon Books, 1989).
15. Vanessa Siddle Walker, *Their Highest Potential: An African American School Community in the Segregated South* (Chapel Hill: University of North Carolina Press, 1996).
16. James Coleman et al., *Equality of Educational Opportunity* (Washington, DC: National Center for Education Statistics, 1966). Today we would call this "achievement gap" an "opportunity gap" and highlight the role of poverty.
17. Katherine Schultz, Patricia Buck, and Tricia Niesz, "Democratizing Conversations: Racialized Talk in a Post-Desegregated Middle School," *American Educational Research Journal* 37, no. 1 (2000): 33–65.
18. Walker, *Their Highest Potential.*
19. Michele Foster, *Black Teachers on Teaching* (New York: New Press, 1997); Schultz, Buck, and Niesz, "Democratizing Conversations"; Walker, *Their Highest Potential.*
20. Gary Orfield et al., Brown *at 62: School Segregation By Race, Poverty, and State* (Los Angeles: The Civil Rights Project, UCLA, 2016), https://www.civilrightsproject.ucla.edu/research/k-12-education/integration-and-diversity/brown-at-62-school-segregation-by-race-poverty-and-state/Brown-at-62-final-corrected-2.pdf.
21. "Virginia's 'Massive Resistance' to School Desegregation," University of Virginia's Digital Resources for United States History, http://www2.vcdh.virginia.edu/xslt/servlet/XSLTServlet?xml=/xml_docs/solguide/Essays/essay13a.xml&xsl=/xml_docs/solguide/sol_new.xsl§ion=essay; Raynard Sanders et al., *Twenty-First Century Jim Crow Schools: The Impact of Charters on Public Education* (Boston: Beacon Press, 2018).
22. Oscar Lewis, *Five Families: Mexican Case Studies in the Culture of Poverty* (New York: Basic Books, 1959).
23. Daniel Moynihan, *The Negro Family: The Case for National Action* (Washington, DC: Office of Policy Planning and Research, United States Department of Labor, 1965).
24. Tyack and Cuban, *Tinkering Toward Utopia.*
25. Geneva Gay, *Culturally Responsive Teaching: Theory, Research, and Practice* (New York: Teachers College Press, 2010); Gloria Ladson-Billings, *The Dreamkeepers: Successful Teachers of African American Children* (Hoboken, NJ: John Wiley & Sons, 2009); Django Paris, "Culturally Sustaining Pedagogy: A Needed Change in Stance, Terminology, and Practice." *Educational Researcher* 41, no. 3 (2012): 93–97.

26. MACOS, or Man: A Course of Study, is a curriculum based on the idea of the spiral curriculum developed by Jerome Bruner, who believed that children could learn any concept and that these concepts should be taught at several ages in increasingly sophisticated ways. MACOS was designed to introduce children to the lives of the Netsilik Inuits, an indigenous group in Canada, in order to help them understand ethnocentrism and racism; https://libguides.ioe.ac.uk/macos.
27. Center for Science, Mathematics, and Engineering Education, "Reflecting on Sputnik: Linking the Past, Present, and Future of Educational Reform," http://www.nas.edu/sputnik/bybee3.htm.
28. National Commission for Excellence in Education, *A Nation at Risk: The Imperative for Educational Reform* (Washington, DC: National Institute of Education, 1983).
29. Jal Mehta, "Escaping the Shadow: 'A Nation at Risk' and Its Far-Reaching Influence," *American Educator* 39, no. 2 (2015): 20.
30. NCEE, *A Nation at Risk*.
31. Mehta, "Escaping the Shadow."
32. Randy Bomer and Beth Maloch, "Relating Policy to Research and Practice: The Common Core Standards," *Language Arts* 89, no. 1 (2011): 38; National Governors Association Center for Best Practices, Council of Chief State School Officers, *Common Core State Standards* (Washington, DC: National Governors Association Center for Best Practices, Council of Chief State School Officers, 2010); Aimee Papola-Ellis, "Teaching Under Policy Cascades: Common Core and Literacy Instruction," *Journal of Language and Literacy Education* 10, no. 1 (2014): 166–187.
33. Jal Mehta, *The Allure of Order: High Hopes, Dashed Expectations, and the Troubled Quest to Remake American Schooling* (Oxford: Oxford University Press, 2013); Jal Mehta, "From Bureaucracy to Profession: Remaking the Educational Sector for the Twenty-First Century," *Harvard Education Review* 83, no. 3 (2013): 463–488; David Hursh, "The Growth of High-Stakes Testing in the USA: Accountability, Markets and the Decline in Educational Equality," *British Educational Research Journal* 31, no. 5 (2005): 605–622.
34. "George W. Bush's Speech to the NAACP," *Washington Post*, July 10, 2000, http://www.washingtonpost.com/wp-srv/onpolitics/elections/bushtext071000.htm.
35. Ibid.
36. Linda Darling-Hammond and George Harrison Wood, *Democracy at Risk: The Need for a New Federal Policy in Education* (Washington, DC: Forum for Education and Democracy, 2008).
37. Claudia Wallis, "No Child Left Behind: Doomed to Fail?" *Time*, June 8, 2008, http://content.time.com/time/nation/article/0,8599,1812758,00.html. Thank you to Anthony Cody for pointing out this argument and article.
38. Jeanne Allen, *Ed Reform IO: Innovation + Opportunity = Results: A Manifesto* (Washington, DC: Center for Education Reform, June 2016), https://www.edreform.com/2016/06/ed-reform-i-o-innovation-opportunity-results-a-manifesto/.
39. Michael Q. McShane, "Only in New Orleans: School Choice and Equity Post-Hurricane Katrina," in *Only in New Orleans*, ed. Luis Mirón, Brian R. Beabout, and Joseph

Boselovic (Rotterdam, Netherlands: Sense Publishers, 2016): 134–135; Sanders et al., *Twenty-First Century Jim Crow Schools.*

40. Janelle Scott, "School Choice as a Civil Right: The Political Construction of a Claim and Its Implications for School Desegregation," in *Integrating Schools in a Changing Society: New Policies and Legal Options for a Multiracial Generation*, ed. Erica Frankenberg and Elizabeth DeBray-Pelot (Chapel Hill: University of North Carolina Press, 2011), 32–35, https://gspp.berkeley.edu/assets/uploads/research/pdf/School_Choice_as_a_Civil_Right.pdf.
41. Ibid.
42. Center on Reinventing Public Education, "National Charter School Research Project 2007," https://www.ewa.org/report/national-charter-school-research-project. It is notable that the charter school movement began with wide-ranging support, including support of the AFT and Albert Shanker.
43. Valerie Strauss, "Cuomo Calls Public School System a 'Monopoly' He Wants to Bust," *Washington Post*, October 29, 20014, https://www.washingtonpost.com/news/answer-sheet/wp/2014/10/29/cuomo-calls-public-school-system-a-monopoly-he-wants-to-bust/?utm_term=.04bfc692bae0; Kate Taylor, "Cuomo, in Shift, Is Said to Back Reducing Test Scores' Role in Teacher Reviews," *New York Times*, November 25, 2015, https://www.nytimes.com/2015/11/26/nyregion/cuomo-in-shift-is-said-to-back-reducing-test-scores-role-in-teacher-reviews.html?ref=topics&_r=1.
44. Strauss, "Cuomo Calls Public School System a 'Monopoly' He Wants to Bust."
45. John E. Chubb and Terry M. Moe, "America's Public Schools: Choice is a Panacea," *Brookings Review* 8, no. 3 (1990): 4–12.
46. David F. Labaree, "Public Goods, Private Goods: The American Struggle over Educational Goals," *American Educational Research Journal* 34, no.1 (1997): 39–81; see Terri Wilson, "Negotiating Public and Private: Philosophical Frameworks for School Choice," chapter 3 in *Exploring the School Choice Universe: Evidence and Recommendations*, ed. Gary Miron, Kevin G. Welner, Patricia H. Hinchey, and William J. Mathis (Charlotte, NC: Information Age Publishing, 2012).
47. Christine Yeh, "Forget Grit. Focus on Inequality," *Education Week*, April 14, 2017, https://www.edweek.org/ew/articles/2017/04/14/forget-grit-focus-on-inequality.html#.
48. Deborah Meier and Emily Gasoi, *These Schools Belong to You and Me: Why We Can't Afford to Abandon Our Public Schools* (Boston: Beacon Press, 2017).
49. Benjamin R. Barber, "Public Schooling: Education for Democracy," in *The Public Purpose of Education and Schooling*, ed. John I. Goodlad and T.J. McMannon (San Francisco: Jossey-Bass, 1997), 22.

Chapter 6

1. Judith Butler, *Frames of War: When is Life Grievable?* (New York: Verso, 2009); Isabell Lorey, *State of Insecurity: Government of the Precarious* (New York: Verso, 2015).
2. Anna Lowenhaupt Tsing, *The Mushroom at the End of the World: On the Possibility of Life in Capitalist Ruins* (Princeton, NJ: Princeton University Press, 2015).

3. Michelle Fine, *Just Research in Contentious Times: Widening the Methodological Imagination* (New York: Teachers College Press, 2017).
4. Margaret Himley, ed., *Prospect's Descriptive Processes: The Child, the Art of Teaching and the Classroom and School* (Prospect Center, 2002); Margaret Himley, with Patricia F. Carini, ed., *From Another Angle: Children's Strengths and School Standards* (New York: Teachers College Press, 2000).
5. Katherine Schultz, "Beginning with the Particular: Reimagining Professional Development as a Feminist Practice," *The New Educator* 7, no. 3 (2011): 287–302.
6. Patricia F. Carini, "How to Have Hope: Play's Memorable Transiency," Talk delivered at the Miquon School, Miquon, PA, 2000.
7. See for instance, Kathleen Riley and Kathryn Solic, "'Change Happens Beyond the Comfort Zone': Bringing Undergraduate Teacher-Candidates into Activist Teacher Communities," *Journal of Teacher Education* 68, no. 2 (2017): 179–192; Kathleen Riley, "Reading for Change: Social Justice Unionism Book Groups as an Organizing Tool," *Urban Education Journal* 12, no. 1 (2015), https://www.urbanedjournal.org/archive/volume-12-issue-1-spring-2015/reading-change-social-justice-unionism-book-groups=organizing-; Kira Baker-Doyle, *Transformative Teachers: Teacher Leadership and Learning in a Connected World* (Cambridge, MA: Harvard Educational Press, 2017).
8. Dale Russakoff, "Schooled," *New Yorker*, May 19, 2014, https://www.newyorker.com/magazine/2014/05/19/schooled.
9. Ibid.
10. David L. Kirp, *Improbable Scholars: The Rebirth of a Great American School System and a Strategy for America's Schools* (Oxford: Oxford University Press, 2015); Sara Mead, "Is Union City a National Model for School Reform?" *Education Week*, February 12, 2013, http://blogs.edweek.org/edweek/sarameads_policy_notebook/2013/02/if_you_havent_yet_you.html; Valerie Strauss, "An Urban School District That Works Without Miracles or Teach for America," *Washington Post*, April 4, 2013, https://www.washingtonpost.com/news/answer-sheet/wp/2013/04/04/an-urban-school-district-that-works-without-miracles-or-superman/?utm_term=.7223ac4071ae; David L. Kirp, "How to Fix the Country's Failing Schools. And How Not To," *New York Times*, January 10, 2016, https://www.nytimes.com/2016/01/10/opinion/sunday/how-to-fix-the-countrys-failing-schools-and-how-not-to.html.
11. Diane Curtis, "A Remarkable Transformation: Union City Public Schools," *Edutopia*, January 24, 2003, https://www.edutopia.org/remarkable-transformation.
12. David L. Kirp, "The Secret to Fixing Bad Schools," *New York Times*, February 9, 2013, https://www.nytimes.com/2013/02/10/opinion/sunday/the-secret-to-fixing-bad-schools.html?login=smartlock&auth=login-smartlock.
13. The Mississippi Freedom Schools were modeled after the secret Citizenship Schools formed in the 1950s by Septima Clark, who established them to teach African Americans literacy skills and knowledge of the Constitution in order to vote. Over several years, Clark started thousands of these schools throughout the south.
14. "Exploring the History of Freedom Schools," *Civil Rights Teaching*, https://www.civilrightsteaching.org/voting-rights/exploring-history-freedom-schools/; Jon N. Hale,

"The Forgotten Story of the Freedom Schools," *The Atlantic*, June 26, 2014, https://www.theatlantic.com/education/archive/2014/06/the-depressing-legacy-of-freedom-schools/373490/.

15. Hale, "The Forgotten Story of the Freedom Schools."
16. "Freedom Schools," Children's Defense Fund, http://www.childrensdefense.org/programs/freedomschools/.
17. Tyrone C. Howard, "Why Black Lives (and Minds) Matter: Race, Freedom Schools and the Quest for Educational Equity," *Journal of Negro Education* 85, no. 2 (2016): 101–113.
18. Jeannie Oakes, Anna Maier, and Julia Daniel, *Community Schools: An Evidence-Based Strategy for Equitable School Improvement* (Washington, DC: National Education Policy Center, June 5, 2017), http://nepc.colorado.edu/publication/equitable-community-schools.
19. Personal communication, October 27, 2015.
20. Sonia Nazario, *Enrique's Journey: The Story of a Boy's Dangerous Odyssey to Reunite with His Mother* (New York: Random House, 2007).
21. Markham recently wrote a powerful account of this phenomenon; see Lauren Markham, *The Far Away Brothers: Two Young Migrants and the Making of an American Life* (New York: Crown Publishing Group, 2017).
22. Caleb Duarte, personal communication, June 28, 2017.
23. Maxine Greene, "Teaching as Possibility: A Light in Dark Times," *Journal of Pedagogy, Pluralism and Practice* 1, no. 1 (1997): 18.
24. Ralph Ellison, *The Invisible Man* (New York: Signet Books, 1952), 16.
25. Patricia F. Carini, *Starting Strong: A Different Look at Children, School, and Standards* (New York: Teachers College Press, 2001), 1.
26. Chimamanda Ngozi Adichie, "The Danger of a Single Story," filmed October 16, 2009, TED video, 18:43, https://www.ted.com/talks/chimamanda_adichie_the_danger_of_a_single_story.

Acknowledgments

Like most of us, I write in conversation with others. Some of these conversations are lengthy and take place over long periods of time. At other times, I might have brief conversations that change my thinking and alter my argumentation. Some of these conversations have been in person, others conducted through written texts. I have been working on this book for several years, which means that there are many people and conversations who have shaped my thinking. As a result, my list of acknowledgments will be too short and invariably leave out important people. I have found that once I focus on an idea (like distrust), I see the whole world through that lens. I apologize to the multitude of people who have put up with having this analysis applied to situations over and over again. Finally, the notion of "acknowledgments" seems like too insignificant a means of expressing the deep appreciation, gratitude, and love I have for the people who have contributed to the ideas in this book. I'll name a few.

First, I want to thank Becca Steinitz, without whose friendship and incredible eye for how to put together ideas and arguments, this book simply would not exist. My husband, David Paul, read each chapter more times than he wanted to, I am sure, and pushed and illuminated many of the ideas, sacrificing a part of every vacation in the past couple of years so that I could write this book. Thea Abu El-Haj brought wisdom and clarity, especially as I neared the finish line. Nancy Feinstein read early chapters and raised critical questions, pushing me to write the book for a wider audience. Cynthia Scheinberg was my writing partner from the beginning and not only helped me get started but also brought incredible intelligence as well as a sense of humor to the project. Melia Repko-Erwin worked with me on the manuscript and especially contributed to my thinking about educational policies. Katie McGinn Luet was instrumental to my writing the chapter on Chester. Alison McDonald's insights about Oakland, introductions, and honesty about my writing was critical to that chapter. Conversations with Thea Abu El-Haj, Dean Brooks, Judy Buchanan, Garene Kaloustian, and Emily Robbins were essential to the writing about our work in Lebanon.

I have had the privilege of many conversations with readers, including Christine Cziko, Caleb Duarte, Joe Dworetsky, Michelle Fine, Susan Jurow, Marvin Hoffman, Amanda Lashaw, Torch Lytle, Lauren Markham, Amy Millikan, Wagma Mommandi, Anna Richert, Rachael Stryker, Rachel Throop, Nancie Zane, and many other people who spent time with me talking about ideas, on the phone or in interviews.

My dear childhood friend, Marianne Jansen Rollinson, who is a talented artist, graciously painted a picture that became the basis of the cover. Her ability to capture complex ideas in color and texture is astounding.

As my editor at Harvard Education Press, Caroline Chauncey has provided valuable advice and insight that shaped the book.

Perhaps most important was the love and support from my family—David, Nora, Danny, and Jenna—who continue to motivate and sustain me every day.

About the Author

Katherine Schultz is Dean and Professor of Education at the University of Colorado Boulder School of Education. Her scholarly work has focused on the research, development, and dissemination of practices that support new and veteran teachers working with marginalized populations in high-poverty areas. Her two recent books, *Listening: A Framework for Teaching Across Differences* and *Rethinking Classroom Participation: Listening to Silent Voices*, address these issues. In particular, she is interested in talking and writing about educational issues for a wide array of public audiences. Since coming to Colorado, one of her areas of focus has been to work with the faculty to develop place-based partnerships including student teaching, professional development, research, policy, and community-engaged projects in three areas: Northeast Colorado, Lafayette (in Boulder County), and the Five Points area of Denver. She has examined and lived the issues of distrust as a teacher, principal, professional development leader, school board member, faculty member, dean, and concerned citizen.

Index

P